Perspectives on Plowden

Edited by Richard Peters

*Professor of the Philosophy of Education,
Institute of Education, University of London*

The school of experience is no school at all,
not because no one learns in it but because
no one teaches. Teaching is the expedition
of learning; a person who is taught learns
more quickly than one who is not.
B. F. Skinner

3|69|16|-

LONDON
ROUTLEDGE & KEGAN PAUL
NEW YORK : HUMANITIES PRESS

First published 1969
by Routledge & Kegan Paul Ltd
Broadway House, 68–74 Carter Lane
London, E.C.4

Printed in Great Britain
by Willmer Brothers Limited
Birkenhead, Cheshire

~~SBN 6359 8 (c)~~ 0-71006359-8
~~SBN 6387 3 (p)~~

THE STUDENTS LIBRARY OF EDUCATION has been designed to meet the needs of students of Education at Colleges of Education and at University Institutes and Departments. It will also be valuable for practising teachers and educationists. The series takes full account of the latest developments in teacher-training and of new methods and approaches in education. Separate volumes will provide authoritative and up-to-date accounts of the topics within the major fields of sociology, philosophy and history of education, educational psychology, and method. Care has been taken that specialist topics are treated lucidly and usefully for the non-specialist reader. Altogether, the Students' Library of Education will provide a comprehensive introduction and guide to anyone concerned with the study of education and with educational theory and practice.

J. W. TIBBLE

Contents

Preface

The papers in this volume arise from discussion about the educational thinking of the Plowden Report. Since they are critical of that thinking we would like to make two preliminary things clear. In the first place we are not attacking the Recommendations of the Report. We refer to them occasionally, but by and large they are not our concern. And although we may have reservations about some of them we certainly believe that by and large they would, if carried out, lead to a marked improvement in primary school education.

In the second place we are anxious that the point and direction of our criticisms shall be understood. We argue that although the general view of education taken in the Report represented a great advance on the more authoritarian thinking that came before it, yet it is theoretically not satisfactory and is far from appropriate to the practical needs of our time. This does not mean that we want a return to the past. Quite the reverse. And we very much respect some of the members of the Plowden Committee and their advisers who have worked for the great improvements that have taken place. We hope indeed that they will not take our criticisms amiss, even when we phrase them a little sharply. For we are very strongly of the opinion that views based on a wider and more exact knowledge of relevant research and a clearer understanding of the distinctive needs of the present and immediate future are now needed. We try to be constructive in our comments, and to point the way to the developments in thinking about the primary school that we would like to see.

It looks now as if many of the Recommendations of the Report may be shelved through lack of finance. Others may seem a bit irrelevant because different decisions were made before the publication of the Report. Nevertheless the Report itself may come to be regarded as an important document on account of the unusual amount of educational theorising that it contains. There is already widespread evidence that it is being treated as an authoritative text-book on the theory of primary education, especially in Colleges of Education. We therefore hope that, if the Report comes increasingly to be treated in this way, our comments on part of it will be read at the same time as a supplement.

The comments are not couched in a form appropriate to a learned journal. Rather they raise points for discussion in a non-technical way and demand little more by way of a background in educational theory than the Report itself. It is to be hoped that they will occasion many discussions and debates on the topics which they raise, and that they will encourage clear thinking, the demand for evidence and the justification of valuative presuppositions which is the hall-mark of good educational discussion. Educational theory has been too much bedevilled in the past by slogans and causes. This monograph is intended to point the way to a more critical empirical approach to these matters that concern us all so much.

Richard Peters

I

'A Recognizable Philosophy of Education': A Constructive Critique

RICHARD PETERS

Professor of Philosophy of Education,
University of London Institute of Education

Introduction

It was understandable about forty years ago that reformers should proclaim that 'education is growth' or that children should be encouraged to learn from experience; for there was a great deal wrong, both morally and psychologically, with the old elementary school tradition. Children were, on the whole, instructed in rather an authoritarian manner with too little respect for their dignity as potential persons and with too little regard to facts about stages of their development, interests, and individual differences. The Hadow Report, in certain celebrated passages, bore witness to this more child-centred approach to education, the intellectual battle for which has now largely been won.

If, however, an educational theory is developed decades later out of such a corrective emphasis without due account being taken of other aspects of the educational situation, a very one-sided and misleading set of beliefs can emerge. My contention is that this has happened with the Plowden Report. I do not refer, of course, to the concrete recommendations which it was the proper business of the committee to make, and do not propose to discuss the case for or against them. I am referring to the little vade-mecum of educational theory to which its readers are gratuitously treated and to which no important recommendations are attached.

Aims – explicit and implicit

The Committee were chary of committing themselves to an explicit statement of aims though they perhaps were not quite clear about the reasons which 'a number of distinguished educationists and professors of educational philosophy' had for cautioning them about them – namely that they must either be highly general and therefore not very informative, such as 'self-realization', or more specific and therefore plural in a society like ours where there are many different convictions about what is important in education. This caution, however, did not save them from blatant contradictions – as when they begin the chapter with a statement of 'one obvious purpose', which is to fit children for the society into which they will grow up, and go on to say later that a school is 'a community in which children learn to live first and foremost as children and not as future adults'. Perhaps this contradiction was not so apparent because it was not in a passage referring explicitly to aims but in one beginning 'A school is . . .' in which a whole ideology is intimated, and called a 'recognizable philosophy of education'. 'Aims' are, by definition, attempts at precision, at explicit emphasis. They involve explicit value-judgments which invite discussion because they are abstracted to guide action. A much more subtle and insidious way of influencing people's attitudes and endeavours is to conceal value judgments in descriptions

2

such as 'the school is . . .'. Another good example of this technique is the loaded and rather saccharine statement which launches Chapter 2: 'At the heart of the educational process lies the child.'

A 'recognizable philosophy of education'

As this section at the end of Chapter 15 on the school contains, in summary form, the implicit ideology of the Report, it is worth quoting in full:

> A school is not merely a teaching shop, it must transmit values and attitudes. It is a community in which children learn to live first and foremost as children and not as future adults. In family life children learn to live with people of all ages. The school sets out deliberately to devise the right environment for children, to allow them to be themselves and to develop in the way and at the pace appropriate to them. It tries to equalize opportunities and to compensate for handicaps. It lays special stress on individual discovery, on first-hand experience and on opportunities for creative work. It insists that knowledge does not fall into neatly separate compartments and that work and play are not opposite but complementary. A child brought up in such an atmosphere at all stages of his education has some hope of becoming a balanced and mature adult and of being able to live in, to contribute to, and to look critically at the society of which he forms a part. Not all primary schools correspond to this picture, but it does represent a general and quickening trend. (Plowden, 1967, Vol. 1 pp. 187-8.)

My contention is that this summary of a 'recognizable educational philosophy' proliferates in important half-truths that are paraded as educational panaceas. It is necessary, therefore, to separate out its various components and to attempt to place them in a more adequate perspective. They are as follows:

(a) That the child has a 'nature' which will 'develop'

if the appropriate environment is provided. What will he develop into? Presumably a 'mature adult' who can 'be himself' and be critical of his society.

(b) Self-direction is very important in this development. 'The child is the agent of his own learning' (Para. 529). 'Sensitivity and observation are called for rather than intervention from the teacher' (Para. 527). Children have an intense interest in the world around them together with powers of concentration which will ensure learning if they are provided with materials for which they are 'ready' (Paras. 533, 534).

(c) Knowledge cannot be divided into separate compartments. Self-chosen activity within an 'integrated curriculum' is desirable.

(d) The teacher must be a guide, an arranger of the environment, rather than an instructor.

At several places in the Report the statement of this dominant ideology is followed by some qualifications – for instance on the importance of 'the older virtues' (Para. 188) or on the dangers in 'discovery methods' (Para. 549, 550). But these read very much like attempts to deal with awkward objections while retaining the main emphasis; they do not add up to an attempt to present a properly thought out educational theory. However, let us look at the details of it under its four main headings, and see to what extent it can form part of a more adequate synthesis.

A constructive critique

Development. What is to be made of the notion that children have a 'nature' or that the individual has a 'self' which will emerge if the right environment is provided? This raises, of course, a host of old questions about what is innate and acquired; but it also raises equally crucial

4

questions about the concept of 'development'. Sometimes, when people talk about 'development', they have in mind a norm which is statistically determined as characterizing children at a certain age in a given society. Stages of physical growth, as plotted by Gesell, can be studied; so can stages of other sorts of 'growth', but the notions of 'growth' and 'development' immediately begin to collect valuative overtones when we pass out of the realm of the purely physical. For is there not lurking even in the fairly colourless notion of 'mental development' some concept of what a man ought to be? Has not a type of norm different from a purely statistical one begun to intrude itself? It manifestly has when words like 'mature' and 'balanced' are introduced.

How is such development to be conceived? In most books on child-development 'development' is divided into physical, intellectual, social, moral and emotional aspects, as if social and moral development were devoid of 'intellect', as if morality and the use of the intellect were free from passion, and as if emotional development was separable from thought and social awareness. This indefensible type of classification should surely be scrapped and replaced by a more logical division into forms of thought and awareness, each of which has its affective aspect. This would include scientific, mathematical, moral, historical, inter-personal, aesthetic, and religious forms of awareness; proper attention should also be paid to the developmental aspects of various forms of skills – 'basic' and linguistic ones included.

What is urgently needed is a new approach to child-development in which the logical aspects of these forms of awareness and the values inherent in them are more closely related to facts about the learning processes of young children. This would imply abandonment of the absurd practice, which is prevalent in Colleges of Education, of curriculum courses being taught either by subject specialists who have little experience of young children or by education lecturers who have experience of young children but only an embryonic knowledge of the subjects. If anything calls for team teaching and the pooling of knowledge, curriculum courses do. Some of the more enlightened Colleges of Education are already moving in this direction.

But even if one tidied up these various aspects of 'development' how would this help to determine the emphasis of education? Is a man more 'developed' if he is highly trained scientifically but aesthetically insensitive or if he is aesthetically sophisticated but a scientific ignoramus? Is a man more developed who is 'well-rounded' but with a thorough knowledge of nothing, than one who is a brilliant mathematician and musician but ignorant of most other things? Was Lenin more 'developed' than Gandhi? And what about the needs of the nation for men suitably trained for the professions, industry, the forces, and the land? How are these pressures to be reconciled with those of 'self-development', however conceived? And what is one to make of this emphasis on being oneself? It is rather like the Existentialist plea that one should be 'authentic'. Out of a context it is a vacuous recommendation which is consistent with any form of development; for presumably the Marquis de Sade was being himself as much as St. Francis. They just had different selves to develop.

There was a time, of course, when forms of awareness were comparatively undifferentiated and when the religious one, in the form of various brands of Christianity, provided some kind of unifying ideal of man against which a man's development could be roughly measured. But those times have passed. We now live in a pluralistic type of society without any such unifying

6

ideal, and as educators we must come to terms with this. Those who stress the importance of individual self-realization as an educational aim are, perhaps unwittingly, lending their support to a pluralist conception of the good life.

As a matter of fact those, like Gesell, who were largely responsible for the ideology of 'growth' and 'development', explicitly linked their doctrine with the democratic ideal of the value of the individual, and contrasted it with alternatives such as Fascism which devalued the individual. In this they were at one with English theorists such as Sir Percy Nunn. Dewey's concept of 'growth', too, was very closely connected with the adventurous initiative of an expanding individualistic society. Nowadays the emphasis on 'growth', and 'self-actualization' by people like Rogers and Maslow is connected very much with the attempt to free the individual from the pressures of social conformity in an 'other-directed' type of society. It is a plea for the individual in a changed social setting.

But what tends to be forgotten by those who identify themselves with this type of ideology is what Dewey called the 'shared experience' which such individual development presupposes. On the one hand there are high-level moral principles such as toleration, respect for persons, fairness, and consideration of people's interests which underpin democratic institutions and which provide the interpersonal framework within which individuals can be encouraged to pursue a variety of interests that are thought to be worth-while. Without some such consensus, into which children must be initiated, the pluralist pursuit of value would be impossible. On the other hand all the different options open to individuals are inescapably social in character. No individual can embark on science, singing or tool-making without being introduced to a vast body of knowledge and skill that has gradually been accumulated, and in most of them he will share a form of life with others who are also engaged on them. Furthermore when we encourage children to be themselves we surely take for granted a vast array of activities and forms of awareness that we think *worthwhile* within which we encourage children to find the ones to which they are particularly suited. As teachers we must make value judgments when we think of any sort of curriculum; for we do not offer blowing up live frogs with bicycle pumps or bingo as possible options. Talk of 'development', like talk of children's 'needs', is too often a way of dressing up our value-judgments in semi-scientific clothes. I will not enter into the difficult discussion of how such value-judgments can be justified; I am only drawing attention to their unavoidable presence. I am arguing that any educator who subscribes to this type of ideology must think that certain types of things are more worthwhile than others, though he may be unwilling to commit himself to comparative judgments within the field of what he thinks is worthwhile. The plea for the development of selves is always to be understood within a framework of shared valuations.

Considerations such as these have led me to wonder more and more whether there is any field of study called 'child development' which can be clearly distinguished from 'education'. Of course there is the physical and physiological side of 'development' with which teachers are not so directly concerned as are doctors and paediatricians. But is mental development distinguishable from 'education'? There was point, at one time, in stressing the separate study of child development because the psychology of children was sadly neglected in decisions about what and how they should be taught. But there is little danger of that nowadays. It will be worthwhile, therefore, to pause a minute to spell out how closely these concepts overlap in order to substantiate my questioning of the case for 'child development' as a separate study.

'Education', as I have argued elsewhere (Peters, 1966, Chs. 1, 2), involves initiation into what is thought to be worthwhile. In stating 'aims' of education we select aspects of what is thought to be worthwhile which we think require special emphasis. The concept of 'development', I have argued, also presupposes value-judgments about what man should be. A study of different developmental theories – e.g. those of Freud, Gesell, or Piaget – reveals slightly different presuppositions about what man should be. They are not 'value-free'.

'Education', secondly, suggests a selection, from what is valuable, of activities and states which involve some depth and breadth of understanding. It is incompatible with passing on a mere know-how and with narrow specialization. 'Education is of the whole man' is a conceptual truth because the concept of 'education' rules out too one-sided development. Now, descriptively speaking, 'development' as an evolutionary concept, involves some degree of differentiation and integration. What else, therefore, can 'mental development' suggest than some differentiation of forms of understanding together with some integration of them? And in what could such 'differentiation' consist if it is not in those forms of understanding which mankind has evolved in order to make sense of the world, to appreciate its many manifold aspects, to control and canalize his inclinations, and to come to terms with his predicament?

Thirdly there is a perennial debate in education theory about the extent to which education comes about through the efforts and influence of teachers, parents, and the peer-group and how much is due to the learner's self-originated activity. Similarly in developmental theories there is a constant debate concerning the respective importance of nature and nurture. It is only if one holds some kind of 'unfolding' theory of development that social influences can be discounted. It is probably because the authors of the section on educational theory in the Report incline towards some kind of 'inner ripening' theory of development that they talk so much about development and children's learning and so little about education and the role of the teacher. And this brings me to the next feature of their 'recognizable philosophy of education' – their stress on the self-direction of the learner.

Self-direction. Obviously enough the stress on self-direction and self-chosen activities is closely connected with the ideal of individual self-development. But it incorporates additional doctrines, one proclaiming a value judgment, the other relating to theories of learning. I will briefly consider each of them in turn.

(i) *Autonomy as a moral principle.* On the one hand a powerful plea is being made for the value of individual autonomy, for the importance attached in a democratic society to individual choice, independence of mind, and to more recondite virtues such as creativeness and originality. I need not expatiate on the importance of this in a pluralist society. But three types of comment are in place. Firstly this, like any other value, must surely be asserted not absolutely but with an 'other things being equal' clause. How far are we going to press the value of self-chosen activities if young people overwhelmingly reject scientific subjects in a highly industralized society which needs increasingly a vast array of technicians and technologists? We may be moving towards such a situation – and it is no good comforting ourselves on the number of young people who seem to be 'choosing' sociology in higher and further education. For we may soon be turning out too many people who can talk knowledgeably in a reformist way about society but too few who can contribute decisively to its economic base. If we think, too, that education is incompatible with narrow specialization how far are we justified in pushing young people into a variety of subjects and activities if they would rather specialize?

Secondly too little is known about how such autonomy independence, and 'creativeness', is developed. It may well be that a very *bad* way of developing this is to give children too many opportunities for uninformed 'choices' too young. One thing, however, is obvious enough – that the notion of 'autonomy' makes very little *sense* unless a child first has a grasp from the inside of what following rules means and has taken rules into himself between which he has to choose. Similarly general talk of 'creativeness' is cant; for there is no such general faculty. One can be creative in science without being a creative cook. And to be 'creative' in any sphere presupposes some mastery of the skills and body of knowledge appropriate to it. As Whitehead wisely put it, the stage of 'generalization' or autonomy comes after the stage of precision. The implication of all these points is that it is essential for children to be initiated into skills and bodies of knowledge which are part of our public heritage, before they can sensibly strike out on their own.

Thirdly, if we accept that there are many ways in which an individual can strike out on his own in a pluralist type of society, and if we think that children should be encouraged to stand on their own feet and find their own way, then we must think seriously about equipping them to do this effectively. This means not only taking them a certain distance in the various options so that they may have experience on the basis of which they may choose; it also means paying special attention to activities such as literature, history, and social studies which are an aid to them in this sort of choice. In Chapter V of *Ethics and Education* I argued that education is pre-eminently concerned with initiating children into activities whose cognitive content spills over into and illuminates other areas of life. I argued that their value derives in part from the fact that they help the individual to answer the question 'What ought I to do?' It is not enough, therefore, to say that children should learn to be themselves at school; we must give them the equipment to find out properly what sort of selves they want to be. In my view the forms of awareness grouped roughly together under the title of 'the humanities' are particularly important in this. It is a hopeful sign that the Schools Council have initiated a special project for providing new kinds of teaching materials in this area.

(ii) *'Discovery' methods*. The doctrine of self-direction relates, on the other hand, to a theory of learning. It suggests that children learn things better if their activities are self-chosen and approximate to 'discovery'. This claim is based almost entirely on teacher's hunches not on objective evidence. As a contributor to the recent American Symposium on the subject put it:

Many strong claims for learning by discovery are made in educational psychology. But almost none of these claims has been empirically substantiated or even clearly tested in an experiment. (Waltrock, 1966, p. 33.)

So much depends, too, on what is being learnt. The learning of skills, for instance, is very different from learning principles and developing attitudes. A great deal of information has to be imparted to a child which he could not possibly discover for himself. The 'discovery' of a bird's nest is obviously very different from discovery in a structured situation like that of Dienes' apparatus. R. F. Dearden has written an excellent article in a recent book making these sorts of points: so there is no need for me to elaborate them any further (Dearden, 1967). There is the further point, too, that *too much* emphasis on self-chosen activities may lead to a certain type of promiscuity amongst children against which Liam Hudson recently warned us in his stimulating book called *Contrary Imaginations* (Hudson, 1966, p. 49). What has happened in this case is a further example of what has happened too often in psychology – *a* method for learning some things has become puffed up into *the* method for learning almost anything. Also the old Aristotelian notion of the entelechy or the self-originated development of an organism, which was so popular with psychologists in the first part of this century, has been transformed, especially in Piaget's theory, into a too exclusive stress on intrinsic motivation.

Non-compartmentalization of knowledge. The committee, predictably enough, made its obeisance to the fashionable view that knowledge cannot be split up into distinct slabs and that the curriculum should therefore be undifferentiated though, interestingly enough, little attention is paid to this conviction when in Chapter 17 'Aspects of the Curriculum' were set out in a traditional way with few suggestions for 'integration'. Again there are important truths in this view, but the various issues need to be disentangled. Firstly though it is perfectly true that many problems require a combination of forms of knowledge for their solution it does not follow from this that distinctions between forms of knowledge are arbitrary. It took acute thinkers such as Hume and Kant a considerable time to establish that mathematics is different from empirical science in important respects and that morals is not really much like either of them. Are we suggesting that philosophers since the seventeenth century have been wrong about such matters? Are we to go back and maintain that religion is indistinguishable from science and that morals is similar to geometrical demonstration? Surely one of the great achievements of our civilization is to have gradually separated out and got clearer about the types of concepts and truth-criteria involved in different forms of thought. But, of course, the different forms of thought make use of each other, once they have been differentiated out. In making moral judgments we would be foolish if we did not make use of science in order to acquaint ourselves better with the facts; scientists use mathematics in order to frame their hypotheses more precisely.

Secondly, in these discussions about the curriculum, forms of knowledge are often confused with school sub-jects which may or may not correspond to pure forms of knowledge. Mathematics and science obviously do; classics and geography obviously do not, and educational theory is, of course, one of the biggest bastards of them all. Whether forms of thought should be taught separ-ately or linked together in some kind of 'topic' or 'pro-ject' approach is a matter which cannot be settled with-out empirical investigation into how successful the various alternatives are in relation to agreed criteria. People who recommend a 'topic' or 'integrated' approach never seem to me clear about the criteria in terms of which their endeavours could be evaluated. Is their rationale a motivational one? Do they think that child-ren – especially early school-leavers – are likely to be less bored by this approach? Is it, in other words, a contain-ment operation to keep children interested while at school – especially when they stay on to sixteen? Or do they think, perhaps, that there is a body of knowledge of a more or less undifferentiated sort that children ought to possess about 'our town', 'power', 'transport' and the like? Or are they really after a kind of moral education, an attempt to sensitize children to certain current issues which they (and perhaps not the children) think important – e.g. race relations, war and peace, and the plight of the aged? Too often, so it seems to me, reformers pass from the undeniable truth that the present 'subject-centred' curriculum is often boring to the conclusion that it should be abandoned and a topic centred one substituted for it. They do not consider sufficiently seriously the less radical suggestion that the more traditional type of curriculum could be both more imaginatively and more realistically interpreted. As with the emphasis on 'discovery' methods one can detect in all this a yearning for some overall recipe for teaching. My contention is that no such overall recipe is possible. What is needed is a down-to-earth, clear-headed, experimental approach which takes due account not only of general criteria but of the differences in what is taught and the children to whom it is taught. I recently went over a primary school where the free-day was in operation. The headmistress sat me down and gave me a long talk about the importance of self-chosen activity and each child working individually on his own curriculum. She then took me straightaway to see a most wonderful class music lesson taken by a professional musician in a formal but relaxed way. The headmistress purred over it – but saw no incompatibility between this lesson and her ideological introduction. But then music is different from reading and people's practices are so often much better than their attempts to relate them to other people's theories!

This brings me to the final point of my critique: *The role of the teacher.* The image of the teacher presented in the Plowden Report is of a child-grower who stands back and manipulates the environment so that children will proceed from discovery to discovery when they are 'ready'. There is so much wrong with this image that one scarcely knows where to begin in criticizing it. Most of what is wrong with it can be summed up by saying that it systematically ignores the inescapably social character of thought and language, of processes of transmission, and of motivation. The notion that children can peel concepts off the world without sensitization to selected aspects of it incorporated in a public language, that most of their interests are self-originated rather than caught from others, that children become 'ready' by some kind of internal ripening without imitation, identification, and instruction – all such notions are highly suspect. Most progressive educators such as Susan Isaacs and Dora Russell worked with small classes of intelligent children drawn predominantly from middle-class homes. I suspect that this idealized picture of the learning situation is largely an extrapolation from such special conditions.

The derogatory impression created by the statement 'The school is not a teaching shop' is again characteristic of this one-sided approach to teaching. For what is teaching? There is masses about learning in the Plowden Report, but almost nothing about teaching. Yet teaching can take the form of instruction, and explanation, of asking leading questions, of demonstrating by example, of correcting attempts at mastery, and so on. It can be done with a whole class, with small groups, and with individuals. Why should all this be associated with a shop? Personally, I always associate the self-chosen type of curriculum with a supermarket, where the teacher stands around benevolently ensuring that the wants of the consumers are satisfied! But more seriously does not the Plowden image of the teacher tend to down-grade

the role of the teacher at a time when the teacher should
be occupying an increasingly important role? For in a
pluralistic society, when there is no unified ideal that
can be handed on by the priests, who else is there to
stand between the generations and to initiate others into
the various aspects of a culture within which the individual has eventually to determine where he stands?
If the teachers are not thought of as, to varying degrees,
authorities on this culture how effective are they likely
to be in a society in which most of the pressures on
young people are not in the direction of education?

I do not want, of course, to deny the effectiveness of
what might be called informal methods in education
generally. I, myself, started my educational career with a
three-year stint in one of the most informal of all educational institutions – a youth centre. When I became a
secondary-school teacher I found it dead-easy compared
with what I had been doing. Ever since, I have retained
the conviction that informal methods, at any level, are
much more demanding of the teacher than more formal
methods. What is demanded is not simply efficiency of
organization and a grasp of what is going on outside the
teaching space, but also knowledge and understanding
that is available at any time – not just after one has
managed to look it all up. I heard of some students recently who were sent to observe an experienced teacher
using informal methods of stimulating children's questions – an admirable way of teaching, if one can man-
age it, in any situation, whether formal or informal. They
were dogged searchers after truth, these students; so they
kept a minute by minute record of what actually transpired in her teaching space. They found that out of thirty
questions demanding an informative answer in a given
period she was only able to deal adequately with five of
them! It is true that she often told the children where

to go and look to find the answers. But most of the children did not bother, and the teacher was usually unable to check on whether they did or not. The reason for this unintentional thwarting of the children's desire to learn was partly the need for controlling the other children and dealing with their constant demands of a non-educational nature; but it was also partly due to the unpredictable demands on the teacher's knowledge in such an unstructured situation. I often wonder whether we are not being altogether too idealistic in expecting many of our teachers to teach continuously in this informal way at the junior school level, let alone in the secondary school. But why should we subscribe to this 'Either-Or' view of teaching at any level?

This is really what I object to most about the Plowden picture of the teacher – its suggestion that there is just one ideal method of teaching, which is usually contrasted with the old formal teaching and 'rote-learning'. I recently encountered this type of ideology at first-hand when I gave a lecture in a College of Education. During the discussion period the following question was put to me out of the blue. 'It is said that the only method of teaching French effectively is to teach the whole class at the same time. Yet it is also said that it is educationally bad to teach the whole class at the same time at the primary level. Should one, therefore, not teach French in the junior school?' I must say that I rather blew up at this point. I said that I did not know either whether this was the only good way of teaching French or whether a case could be made on general grounds for teaching French in the junior school. But if there were good reasons for teaching French and if this was the best way of teaching it, then, in heaven's name why not teach it this way? The acid test, after all, was whether the children learnt anything. At this point there was a cry of

'Heresy' from the audience. It transpired that the last thing that many of the students were encouraged to do was to *experiment* with teaching methods to see which were best from the point of view of children's learning!

This, I fear, is the plight which we are in in many centres of education in this country – locked in the embrace of a constricting ideology. The prevailing pattern of teacher training has been to supplement a basic training in subjects and the handing on of skills by an attempt to bring about commitment to some sort of ideology. This was peculiarly appropriate to small single-sex colleges staffed largely by dedicated women. The time for this is now passing. Colleges are getting much larger and mixed; there are problems of discipline and consensus; and all sorts of new ideas are flowing into them. The educational system of the country is in a highly fluid state; there is little agreement about the aims of education; the curriculum is everywhere under discussion; teaching methods are constantly being queried and the lack of established knowledge about their effectiveness is becoming patent to any serious student of education.

In a situation like this any cosy ideology is not only an irrelevance; it can also positively hamstring a teacher. I heard of a case a few weeks ago where a student dutifully set up an interest table in one of our tougher types of London school. The children calmly swiped the lot. The supervisor complained to the head who remarked that he had put the student in the best-behaved class in the school and that the children in this school were not ready for those sorts of methods. 'But I cannot give up my principles' protested the lecturer. But *Half Our Future* has a past which renders them initially unresponsive to methods more suitable to children emerging from middle-class homes, which provide not only plenty of language and materials, but also attitudes favourable to learning and a system of social control that is responsive to individual differences. If we are going to be child-centred, for heaven's sake let us actually study the children whom we have to teach.

The moral of all this is not, of course, that we should throw overboard all that has been learnt from 'progressive' methods and revert to archaic systems of undiluted mass instruction. It is rather that we should do all in our power to help teachers to develop a critical, empirical, adaptable attitude to methods of teaching and encourage them to learn to think on their feet and experiment with different ways of teaching different types of subjects to different types of children. If only this critical, experimental attitude to teaching could be more encouraged we might soon cease to turn out teachers who thought that if they can only keep talking – or stop talking – then children are necessarily learning something, or teachers who practice something approximating to a free day without keeping a careful check on what in fact each child has learnt. Better still, we might turn out no teachers for whom 'teaching' has become a dirty word.

2

The Aims of Primary Education

ROBERT DEARDEN

Lecturer in Philosophy of Education
University of London Institute of Education

*Plowden on aims**

Out of its five hundred and fifty-five pages, the Plowden Report devotes just three and a half to a discussion of aims. (The Gittins Report, in devoting no more than a single paragraph to aims, even more nearly approaches silence on this subject.) A substantial part of even that tiny portion is devoted to doubts, not quite as to whether it is right actually to *have* any aims, but as to whether there is anything to be gained from trying to state them. 'General statements of aims,' the Report says, 'tend to be little more than expressions of benevolent aspiration which may provide a rough guide to the general climate of a school, but which may have a rather tenuous relationship to the educational practices that actually go on there' (para. 497).

It may be agreed at once that this depressing verdict is true enough of some statements of aim. It would be

* In writing this and the following section I have drawn material from my book *The Philosophy of Primary Education*, Routledge & Kegan Paul, 1968.

true, I think, of the favoured phrases of child-centred theorists, if those phrases are taken to be expressive of *aims*, rather than of general teaching *procedures* (see Peters, 1964, Sec. 2). In fact, it seems to be just such phrases that the Committee did have in mind. They preface their depressing verdict with the lament that 'phrases such as "whole personality", "happy atmosphere", "full and satisfying life", "full development of powers" ... occurred again and again' (para. 497).

Then what might a good statement of aim look like? From the depressing verdict about statements of aim that has been quoted, one might infer that a good statement would accurately describe what actually goes on in the schools. For a good statement of aims, apparently, should be a guide to, and be other than tenuously related to, 'the educational practices that actually go on there'.

But that would be to leave everything as it is: the long-standing habits, the conventions, the confusions, the uncertainties, and practices that have outlived their usefulness. It would simply be to give a pleasing decoration to a well established and autonomous tradition. A quotation from Dewey is apposite here: 'The traditional school could get along without any consistently developed philosophy of education. About all it required in that line was a set of abstract words, like culture, discipline, our great cultural heritage, etc., actual guidance being derived, not from them, but from custom and established routines' (Dewey, 1938, ch. 2).

Yet if there is one thing that is true about primary education today, it is surely that there is no such clearly established tradition to rely on. The old elementary school tradition was clear enough about what the teacher was supposed to do. It arranged a concerted programme of mutually supportive teaching, and it provided institutional support for all the measures that a teacher might have to take. But today that tradition is, quite rightly, in process of rapid eclipse. With this eclipse the concept of the primary school has become somewhat clouded, and the teachers somewhat uncertain.

There are, of course, some who are ready to talk approvingly of 'good teachers', 'good practices', and 'good learning situations', as if what was 'good' just *showed* itself, and as clearly and unambiguously to all as does what is square, or four-footed. The evaluative 'good', however, implies criteria which, characteristically, remain only implicit and hence unexamined. Yet to take such criteria for granted, and not to become conscious of them and of their foundation, if such exists at all, is precisely what one cannot do in times of rapid change like the present, when traditional practices are being brought wholesale into question, and when reforms of doubtless value are, equally doubtlessly, being intermixed with gimmickry and hobby-horses. It is precisely the general evaluative criteria of what is 'good' which need attention, if the constant flood of recommendations, innovations, and advice from all sides, are to be sifted, assessed, and intelligently adapted to local circumstances. In short, we need to reflect a little on our aims.

A good statement of aims, then, is badly needed, and yet cannot simply be an accurate guide to what already actually goes on. In any case, no coherent score could be written for that part of the performance when individuals are all tuning up their separate instruments. And nor will it do, as Plowden rightly implies, to produce as statements of aim the vague phrases of child-centred theory, whatever their merits may be in giving procedural guidance. Nevertheless, it seems to me that statements of aim must be general. This is not a fault about them but surely precisely their function. They have to provide

c

overall orientation and direction for a highly complex activity, which is what I take education to be. It is not the function of statements of aim to settle all the details of organization and method, which would be very much an interdisciplinary matter, but to set out the general objectives which this organization and these methods are to subserve.

One further criticism of Plowden on aims deserves mention. The Plowden Report is a work of *recommendation*, and hence logically cannot avoid assuming certain things to be educationally valuable. If it does not state the aims expressive of these values, still it will not have escaped actually having them. They will simply lie, implicit only and therefore unexamined, scattered through the body of its recommendations.

One example may be produced to show that this is indeed so. At the beginning of chapter two, one hundred and eighty pages away from the chapter on aims, and embodied in a mass of empirical research, lurks the following statement: 'At the heart of the educational process lies the child. No advances in policy, no acquisitions of new equipment, have their desired effect unless they are in harmony with the nature of the child, unless they are fundamentally acceptable to him' (para. 9).

This sheer assertion, which is in no way derivable from the empirical research in which it is embedded, is in reality a major policy statement. Yet it assumes: (i) that the child has a 'nature', which is a dubious metaphysical assertion; (ii) that we ought to adopt the principle of always starting from and being acceptable to this 'nature', which is an unargued ethical recommendation.

This is just one example, but a very important one, of how the refusal to reflect upon aims does not allow one to escape from actually having them, but simply begs a whole lot of questions by leaving them implicit and unexamined. The structure of the move is this: do not actually state your aims in a way which draws close attention to them, but, at a lower level, enter into discourse which can in fact be engaged in only if such aims are tacitly presupposed; then people will be so absorbed in the conversation that they will not notice that the train is moving off in the desired direction.

However, although it seems to me that there is justice in these criticisms which I have made, it would be unjust to ignore the fact that the Plowden Report does actually have something explicit to say about aims, even though what it says is rather meagre and unsystematized. The Report's references to learning by discovery, to being creative and to 'being oneself' all obliquely draw attention to the fundamental value of individual autonomy. This is a value which was brought squarely to the forefront, at least in ethical theory, by Kant in 1785. In relation to intellectual understanding it was implicit in the methodic doubt of Descartes, set out in his *Discourse on Method* and *Meditations*, published in the seventeenth century. Lively awareness of this value in educational practice is, however, quite a recent phenomenon.

In addition to these implicit references, a hint and a caution are also offered by the Committee. The hint is that our children will eventually grow up to live in a society which will require them to be adaptable workers and discriminating consumers, and which will provide them with leisure to fill and others to live with. As to the caution, this is to the usual effect that 'knowledge does not fall into neatly separate compartments' (para. 505). But perhaps we need not take this caution too seriously, since the Report itself then proceeds to a discussion which is divided into eleven separate and conventional subject compartments (ch. 17).

Religion and aims

But valuable and constructive as criticism is, since to see that something is false is in fact to grow in one's knowledge, it does not by itself furnish the positive statement of aims which I suggested that we require. A fresh start might therefore be made with the problem of values which is at the bottom of all this by noticing a feature of the concept of education itself. 'Education', in its most unrestricted sense, seems to mean the processes of learning by means of which people are brought to an understanding and appreciation of what is valuable in human life. 'Education' is, therefore, as Professor Peters has argued in the first chapter of his *Ethics and Education* (Peters, 1966), an evaluative concept. Only ironically do we refer to learning which changes people for the worse as being 'education'. But it is also a formal concept like 'good' itself, in that it leaves the value-content largely undetermined.

In the past, of course, a major value-orientation has been provided by religion, which has presented a system of beliefs about God, man and the world, together with various prescriptions thought consequent upon those beliefs as to how one should conduct oneself. And formal education has, therefore, in the past been orientated by religious doctrine. The elementary school itself, as Plowden points out (para. 493), partly derived from the National Society for the Education of the Poorer Classes in the principles of the Established Church.

This religious influence on primary education remains: in the legal compulsion to hold some form of communal school worship, in the holding of classroom prayers, in the giving of religious instruction, in the convention of the Reports of always placing religion first in curricular recommendations (a convention broken by the Gittins Report, which accords first place to Welsh), and in the often expressed sentiment that religion should pervade the whole of school life.

Nevertheless, the teaching of religion in state schools, which in practice most children must compulsorily attend, is now raising acute problems. The meaning and truth of religious doctrines are more and more being brought into question by people who take the trouble seriously to reflect on them. And if, as is quite indisputable, the truth of those doctrines is seriously doubted and on excellent grounds, then it must be regarded as an objectionable form of indoctrination to propagate these doctrines in the schools *as if* they were unquestionably true.

Furthermore, prayer and worship are hollow, meaningless activities unless certain things are believed about the object to whom they are addressed, namely God. Such activities are in fact logically impossible apart from the presupposition of an actual belief in God. This is not to deny, of course, that the externals of prayer and worship can be compelled, or to deny that those who will not pray can be punished with detention, as sometimes happens in secondary schools. But this is something that could be regarded as justifiable only by one who esteemed cynicism a virtue.

None of this is any objection at all to teaching children *about* religion, which need imply on one's own part only a belief about what others believe. An atheist could teach *about* religion without any loss of intellectual integrity, just as a religious person could teach *about* Marxism or atheism. But at the moment, primary school teachers often go far beyond this, both in indoctrinating their questionable beliefs and in initiating children into their religious practices.

Religious indoctrination, as opposed to teaching *about*

religion, is incompatible with respect for personal autonomy. It is so, not only in trying to produce unshakeable
beliefs in what is in fact only questionably true, but
also in positively encouraging dependence on authority
for what one is to believe. A characteristic and apparently shameless inconsistency in much of child-centred
theory is that it advocates respect for autonomy, for instance by encouraging questioning, testing truth for oneself, and critical acceptance of beliefs, but only to capi-
tulate to authoritarianism in the face of religion. As
Plowden puts it, in a sentence which I personally find
distressing, children 'should not be confused by being
taught to doubt before faith is established' (para. 572).
Should children ask awkward questions, then Plowden
recommends, apparently as just one amongst a choice of
several possible alternatives, that 'they should be given an
honest answer' (para. 572), and that the teacher should
not 'try to conceal from his pupils the fact that others
take a different view' (loc. cit.).

To all of this the obvious counter is that there is still
a majority of parents, and of primary even if not of
secondary teachers, who agree to the suggestion that
religion should continue to be taught. The Plowden Report says that this is so as part of its evidence. In reply
to this it is worth pointing out that only about one-fifth
of these supporters are also in favour of their own active
church membership. Furthermore, being in favour of
'teaching religion' is thoroughly ambiguous as between
teaching *about*, and indoctrinating.

Another point is that one does not have here a principle of argument on which a case is being rested, but
just a handy stick with a certain usefulness. For elsewhere in the Plowden Report, in connection with corporal punishment, the same majorities are cited, in fact
absolutely overwhelmingly and convinced majorities in

this case, but the *contrary* conclusion is drawn. Here, the Report says, 'we believe ... that the primary schools, as in so much else, should lead public opinion, rather than follow it' (para. 750).

But if there is one thing that a principle of argument will not allow, it is having the conclusion whichever way currently happens to suit one's interests. As Professor O'Connor puts it, one cannot 'claim the benefits of reason without acknowledging its risks' (O'Connor, 1957, 125).

Values and the curriculum

The position to which we come, then, is this. Education implies processes of learning in which we come to understand and appreciate what is valuable in human life. But about what *is* valuable there is endless dispute, including now, and on an extensive scale, dispute about religion as a possible answer to the question of values. As between these differing values and ideals of life the state schools, which in practice the majority of children are legally compelled to attend, ought not to be partisan. There are other educational agencies, such as the family, church and Sunday School, or even the extra-curricular parts of the school's own provision, which can present partisan views to those who can be persuaded to listen to them. But having said that much, one's problem then is to see what is left from which to construct a common curriculum. There are, I shall argue, at least two valid, and partly overlapping, approaches to this problem.

First approach. The first approach is to recall that, in spite of the fact that our society is pluralist in regard to values, there does remain a quite substantial and acceptable consensus on what is basically valuable for personal and social competence in our form of life. These are the things hinted at in Plowden when the Committee mentions the society into which our children will eventually grow up. What is involved here is perhaps all rather obvious, but I will briefly spell it out.

To begin with, there is the importance of being economically viable, which points at the very least to a constantly revised component in the curriculum of traditional linguistic and arithmetical skills. Next, there is living with others in a justly ordered form of social life, which points, perhaps to social science, and certainly to some form of basic moral education. Again, there is the worthwhile use of leisure, which would point to a rich range of optional extra-curricular activities, such as field games, and clubs and societies, both religious and secular. Furthermore, there is the enjoyment of physical and mental health, which points to physical education and also to an informed sensitivity in teacher-pupil relationships and in general classroom arrangements. Finally, there are valued forms of personal relationship, such as those of love, family life and friendship, which point to several things, including perhaps sex education, 'domestic science' and moral education once again.

This first approach, then, of inquiring into the basic necessities of personal and social competence, can be made to yield a limited set of aims and corresponding curricular recommendations. But the result is clearly minimal, and certainly would not normally occupy the whole of primary schooling, still less the full ten years of compulsory schooling. Some further basis for enriching the school's programme is therefore clearly necessary.

Second approach. The second approach that I mentioned is, perhaps, rather less obvious, but nevertheless very fruitful. It stems from the view I put forward that state schools ought not to be partisan as between the various differing but morally acceptable ways and ideals of life, differing choices of how to live, to be found in our pluralist society. Compatibly with maintaining a basic level of morality, we may choose a life of scholarship, or pursuit of the arts, or active membership of some church, or being close to nature, or family life and intimate friendships, or risk and adventure – or a life of some combination of these and many other valued activities. The logic of this situation must force upon the school the view that children should choose for themselves what suits them best and where their loyalties are to lie.

To present the matter in this way is to say that we will indeed choose, and not just plump for, or be told what to believe and do. And this is already to take for granted the value of personal autonomy which I detected earlier behind a number of Plowden's proposals. There are two aspects to such an autonomy, one negative and one positive. The negative aspect is that of independence of authorities who dictate what we are to believe, or direct us in what we are to do. The complementary positive aspect is, first, that of testing the truth of things for ourselves, whether by experience or by a critical estimate of the testimony of others, and secondly, that of deliberating, forming intentions, and choosing what we shall do, according to a scale of values which we can ourselves appreciate.

Even for us to question whether all this is so is already to take for granted that it is we who will decide the merits of the answer, not someone else in authority over us. But the positive value of personal autonomy is not revealed by the logical invulnerability which it has, on account of the paradoxes involved in questioning it. We may have been brought up so to respect authority that the very idea of asserting such autonomy would now strike us as wicked, or at least as very ill-advised. We may have been brought up in something like the elementary school tradition at its most authoritarian, with obedience and deference made into second nature. The positive value of personal autonomy is revealed rather in such things as intellectual and moral integrity, in the security and confidence of having a reasonably coherent and well-founded understanding of our situation in the world, and in the satisfaction of exercising a responsible, personal agency.

If personal autonomy is indeed of such fundamental importance among values, then it is most highly deserving of respect, in others by us and in us by others. Furthermore, such a value will be rich in the guidance which it gives over the procedures to be adopted in teaching. For if understanding for ourselves and responsible agency are constitutive of autonomy, then methods of teaching should be devised which bring about such an understanding and which cultivate such a sense of personal agency. Vague notions such as 'the needs of the child' now begin to get some specification and backing. 'Starting from interests' recommends itself as one possible approach that does not call for authoritarian imposition and overruling. And development in the direction of greater autonomy would seem to me to be the valuable heart in such child-centred doctrines as that children should 'grow', that they should 'learn by discovery', and that they should be allowed to choose and to do as much as possible for themselves. (This concept is not entirely without qualification. See R. S. Peters' paper in this volume).

But if personal autonomy is indeed of fundamental importance among values, this is already to admit there to *be* other values. Granted that it is I who am to understand and choose, then what is worth understanding, and what deserves to be chosen? The curriculum problem now shows itself to have been far from solved by the

acceptance of the procedural principle of respect for autonomy, for how is account of these other values to be
taken? If it is in teaching subjects, then which subjects?
If in developing interests, then which interests are to be
encouraged or stimulated, and what is it for them to
'develop'? And if the teacher does not take it upon himself to direct the whole of the proceedings, mistakes and
unwise choices will sometimes be made, and effort will
sometimes be misdirected. Such mistakes may be acceptable, on a long-term view, as the inevitable accompani-
ments of gaining independence, but up to what point are
they acceptable? A teacher is as much responsible for
what happens if he withdraws as if he intervenes.

These procedural difficulties arise, of course, because
young children cannot be regarded as fully fledged autonomous agents, in relation to whom the teacher can properly be seen as no more than advisory. Autonomy is
something progressively developed, not something given,
full-blown, from the start, and such that choice of activities should properly only be negotiated with children.
Furthermore, it is simply an assumption, not a patent
truism, that abundant free choice does in fact develop
autonomy better than does a measure of teacher direction. This is not, I hope, an implicit apology for authoritarianism, but the questioning of a permissiveness
which rightly sees the fundamental value of personal
autonomy, but which cannot see the value of anything
else.

To summarize this second approach as so far presented,
then, I have argued from a recognition of the fact that
choices have to be made between ideals and ways of life,
and from an acceptance of the principle that the public
school ought not to be partisan as between these choices.
The first implication to be drawn from this is the important tautology that if I am to *choose*, then *I* am to

choose. That is to say, the logic of the situation forces personal autonomy into prominence as a value. But the choices actually made will themselves scarcely be of any value unless they are made with as great a degree as possible of understanding of what the situation is and of the possibilities it contains.

Choice and understanding. To begin to develop this last point, I want to introduce here the notion of a 'form of understanding', which immediately shows itself to be a notion connected with knowledge and experience. (I have particularly in mind here, and am greatly indebted to, the views developed by Professor P. H. Hirst in his influential article 'Liberal Education and the Nature of Knowledge' in *Philosophical Analysis and Education*, edited by R. D. Archambault, Routledge and Kegan Paul, 1965). There are two aspects of forms of understanding which are important here. First, they are systems of interconnected concepts and organizing principles. Secondly, they have distinctive validation procedures for determining the truth, rightness, or adequacy of various statements or judgments that may be made.

Before going further, however, let me remove three possible misconceptions. What I have in mind as a 'form of understanding' is certainly not what I like to call the 'rucksack' theory of knowledge. The 'rucksack' theory of knowledge is the theory that knowledge is just a jumbled mass of information such as might be exhibited to advantage on a quiz programme. The two relevant features in the analogy are that rucksacks can be more or less full, and that they are loosely carried behind. The knowledge embraced in a form of understanding, however, is organized, well-founded, and so ingredient in the mind as to transform, not just supply more information about, one's experience.

Next, understanding is not just a single, monolithic and

undifferentiated whole, but is of several quite distinct and non-arbitrary forms. Far from being a seamless robe, such knowledge is better thought of as a coat of many colours, or at any rate a coat of at least five colours. The basis of division between those various forms is not just tradition, or a formal teacher's love of 'watertight compartments', but is to be found in the nature of such knowledge and experience itself. It is to be found, as Professor Hirst and others have shown, in the different sorts of concepts involved, and in the different kinds of reason-giving which are appropriate in validation of judgments made.

The third possible misconception that I want to remove is that the development of such forms of understanding is just a matter of good attitudes, together with possession of a universal information-getting skill. The gratifyingly simple, but unfortunately also simple-minded, view is now abroad that knowledge is really no great thing. Rather than 'top up pots' or 'plaster on facts' – and it is usually in such depreciative terms as these that gaining knowledge is described – how much better to develop good attitudes. For if one has good attitudes towards knowledge, even though one does not actually possess it, one need only deploy the universal information-getting skill in order to be as well placed as the next man. There is, of course, point in this as a reaction against the elementary school tradition of memorization and drill, but it has a grossly over-simple view of how much is to be learned just by opening one's eyes or turning the pages of a book.

Forms of understanding, then, are distinguished by their concepts and their validation procedures, or, if you like, by the ways in which they answer the questions 'What do you mean?', and 'how do you know?' In grasping these concepts and procedures our experience is gradually transformed, and new realities are disclosed which extend and enrich our understanding of our situation in the world. They show us what 'the world' *is*. Each of these forms has its own style of critical thinking, its own ways of being creative and of exercising imagination, and its own ways of refining feeling and guiding activity. These forms are, I suggest, and with the primary school in mind, mathematics, science, history, the arts and ethics.

The answer to the question 'How do you know that $23 \times 12 = 276$?' is to be found in a way quite different from finding the answer to the question 'Are these the remains of a Roman camp?' Again the question 'Don't you think that the figures in this picture are badly distributed?' is not to be found by performing a controlled laboratory experiment. Nor is the rightness or wrongness of bullying or lying to be judged by an exercise of our aesthetic sensitivities. Of course, hardheaded men are often depreciative of anything except mathematics and science, and may regard history, the arts and ethics as no more than carnivals of subjectivity. But why should everything be judged by the standards of mathematics and science? Why not heed Aristotle's caution, in the *Nichomachean Ethics*, when he suggests as one mark of an educated man that in any subject he looks only for so much precision as its nature permits?

To draw all this together then: the exercise of choice which is the expression of one's autonomy presupposes a well-grounded understanding of one's situation in the world. Such an understanding in turn is neither just having a load of information loosely carried behind, not is it just having good attitudes, together with an information-getting skill of mythical potency. It is rather an insight into certain basic ways in which human experience has, as a matter of historical fact, been developed and elaborated.

The claim is not that *all* knowledge is of one or other of these forms. Primitive abilities such as knowing how to raise one's arm, or how to locate sensations, are not included, nor are the more everyday sorts of perception and memory, such as the perception that this is a flower, a farm or a frying pan, or the recollection that I had eggs for breakfast last Monday. Nor is it claimed that every one of these forms of understanding enters into every choice that anyone ever makes.

The claim is rather this. First, these forms of understanding are structural of what have historically turned out to be very wide-ranging modes of experience, and hence are basic ingredients in one's understanding of one's situation in the world. Secondly, as such they are relevant to very many, and probably to all of the more important, choices that we have to make, both in our work and in our leisure. And thirdly, their consequent essential connection with the exercise of personal autonomy, together with the requirement of a systematic schooling for their development, make them obviously central candidates for education in the curriculum of our primary schools.

It is also politically necessary that they should be included, as was not done in the elementary school tradition. The importance of these forms of understanding is shown by the zeal with which defenders of selfish privilege deny access to them to those they wish to keep in bondage. As Robert Lowe, architect of much in the elementary school tradition, put it: the lower classes ought to be educated to discharge the duties cast upon them. And nor will one's sense of injustice at this fitting of people for suitably menial and impoverished lives be nowadays removed by reference to the stations to which it has pleased God to call them.

The Primary School curriculum

The aims and curriculum for the primary school at which one arrives, then – and in suggesting these I am not attempting a straight deduction, so much as exercizing a certain practical judgment in the light of the two approaches I have described – is as follows. First of all, there would be made at least a beginning in developing an understanding of mathematics, science, history and the arts. Mathematics and the arts would be introduced from the start, in the infant school, while science and history, as distinct from the rovings of a promiscuous and uninstructed natural curiosity, would probably best be left until the second year or so of the junior school. I cannot myself see any justification for dividing further either the sciences or the arts at the primary stage. At some point in the primary school, what *we* know to be physics, chemistry, biology, meteorology, geology, astronomy and physical geography would all be touched upon, as would elementary anthropology, economic geography and some aspects of the psychology of perception. But there seems to be absolutely no point in making explicit these ponderous distinctions.

Where the arts are concerned there seem to be great advantages, in addition to having the truth, in an explicit recognition that they belong together as aspects of aesthetic education. I have in mind here poetry, 'creative writing', drama, singing, instrumental music, dancing, painting, drawing and clay modelling as examples of the relevant aspects of aesthetic education. The advantage of recognizing their common contribution to aesthetic understanding is that by tying them together in this way it makes it much less easy for perpetuators of the elementary school tradition to ignore them, in the pursuit of

'English and arithmetic', or something of that sort. It also helps to direct attention to these activities themselves, so that poetry is not treated just as a spring board for a geography lesson, drawing is not treated as a chance to do some more geometry, and painting and drama are not regarded just as occasions for some lay psycho-analysis.

In drawing up an actual syllabus, of course, further sub-criteria would be needed. These might include: (i) logical priority; (ii) the particular interests shown by children; (iii) special knowledge and abilities of staff; (iv) utility in relation to some other part of the curriculum; (v) economic value; (vi) exemplification in our own particular form of social life or local area. Doubtless there would also be other such sub-criteria.

The second major component in the primary school curriculum would be the 'basic skills'. These would include the mechanics of reading and writing, perhaps learning to speak a foreign language, learning to speak English in the case of immigrants, some of the Welsh, and some English children, a constantly reviewed amount of social arithmetic, and finally, I think also map-reading ought now to be included as a basic skill of high utility.

The third component would be physical education in its various aspects. This would include activities of a gymnastic kind, team-games, swimming, some athletics and also some incidental health and sex education, both of which at this pre-adolescent stage might well be treated as sub-criteria in the choice of topics for science.

Fourthly, there could well be a wide range of extra-curricular activities which a primary school might arrange. These might include chess, stamp, and art and craft clubs as well as outdoor games, though this would all be an optional matter for children and staff alike, of course.

So far I have said nothing concrete about the fifth of the forms of understanding that I mentioned earlier, namely ethics. It would seem best for this to enter into primary education mainly through other activities rather than as a formally structured piece of learning on its own, and hence would be shown in the procedural principles adopted. Fundamental amongst these, I argued, should be respect for personal autonomy. But autonomy is enhanced in value as we increase in our understanding and appreciation of other sorts of value, which ought not to be depreciated in a one-sided adulation of 'the child'. Doing justice all round here poses nice problems of judgment for the teacher, problems which could be thought to be solved in advance of all circumstances only by the doctrinaire.

In addition to respect for autonomy, I take also to be included under ethics such general moral principles as fairness and consideration of interests, and such more particular specifications of these as have to be made explicit as rules. Many more particular moral rules, however, can remain implicit at this stage, as part of a general climate of expectation regarding acceptable standards of behaviour. (I have attempted a much more extended discussion of moral education at the primary stage in the book referred to at the beginning of this paper (Dearden, 1968).)

Beyond such a basic morality as this, the ethical includes also a multitude of more or less divergent ideals and ways of life, and hence of possible self-concepts in terms of which to identify oneself and to achieve integrity. Here, on the views which I have presented, the teacher's task is not that of firm insistence but of the disclosure of possibilities. Such a disclosure of ways and modes of life should not be accompanied by subtle, or often very unsubtle, pressures towards compliance and initiation, but should take place through history, including the history of religion, literature, including religious literature, and also those aspects of science concerning men and how they live.

Finally, it seems to me that there is really no such thing as *primary* education, if by that is meant anything more than an administratively and developmentally convenient *stage* in an education which is one. The education which is given in the primary school must therefore always be incomplete and cannot be autonomous. The success of the primary school is to have made a good start.

3

Other Aspects of Child Psychology

BRIAN FOSS

*Professor of Psychology, Bedford College,
University of London. Formerly Professor of
Educational Psychology, University of London
Institute of Education*

Introduction

Psychology is most precise when predicting behaviour in
rather artificial controlled situations, and much less precise over the everyday behaviour with which education
is concerned. It is not easy to make predictions with
enough certainty to be useful to the authors of the Plowden Report. Indeed the Report's recommendations could
have been arrived at without considering any psychological evidence at all. Nothing that is said in this chapter will reflect on those recommendations. Rather the
intention is to fill out the psychological background.

The authors of the psychological sections have said
rather little about teaching and learning, but dwelt rather
on some parts of psychology which are relevant to a
child's all round development, and specifically to the
development of personality. In doing this they have con-
centrated particularly on the younger children (indeed
on the pre-school child) and said almost nothing about,
for instance, the social pressures which are so influential
on older children in the Primary age range. This emphasis

is doubtless based on the contention (which may well be correct) that the early years are the formative ones. In theorizing and collecting evidence about these early years, educational psychologists tend to fall into two groups. The larger group favours a Freudian or Jungian or Kleinian framework, tending to take a clinical approach in studying 'the whole child', and using ideas such as unconscious processes and family relationships in describing the child's development; while an understanding of cognitive rather than emotional or personality development depends on a study of Piaget's work. In contrast, there are those who prefer a more experimental psychological viewpoint, who look at development in terms of learning (in the wide sense of modification of behaviour through experience), and who may use one or more of the so-called theories of learning as a frame of reference. This kind of psychology is often more rigorous; its main disadvantage is that it does not help the teacher to view the child 'as a whole', and indeed gives the impression that the child is a plastic and passive lump moulded by his environment. Despite this, experimental psychology is able to contribute, and the Report has underestimated this contribution.

Before attempting to redress the balance, may I comment on some of the evidence which has been adduced.

Imprinting and critical periods

The report (p. 12) overstates the characteristics of the phenomenon known as imprinting, and refers to the idea that some kinds of imprinting can only occur during certain 'critical periods'.

The implication of the term 'critical period' is that there are certain periods during a person's life which are particularly favourable for learning specific things. Better terms are 'sensitive period' and 'optimal learning period', which imply less clear cut-off points. Such periods can be regarded as having an onset and an offset. Before the onset, the particular kind of learning cannot occur; after the offset, something happens which makes the learning impossible, or more difficult, or just less efficient.

The following are examples of psychological phenomena to which the terms can be applied. John Bowlby (1953) has considered that the first years of life (and particularly the second half of the first year) are particularly important for the development of an attachment between an infant and his mother. The onset of the period is at about five months, since before then the infant does not discriminate mother from others. The reasons for the offset of the period are not clear, but Bowlby considers that if an attachment is not formed during this time, the infant will grow into a person who can never form good affectional bonds. By contrast 'reading readiness' puts emphasis on the onset of a period, whereas the idea that language cannot be learned later in life emphasizes the offset.

The concepts are based on work done originally with animals.

a. If dogs are reared in a 'deprived' environment for the first months, they will later be unsociable, poor at solving problems and slow to adapt to noxious stimuli, as compared with dogs reared normally.

b. Chimpanzees reared in the dark for the first six months appear later to be very slow in visual learning.

c. Birds whose flying is prevented for too long do not learn to fly.

d. According to Lorenz (1937), some birds (e.g. goslings) follow the first moving objects they see and become 'imprinted' on them. He thought that this form of early learning determined the choice of sexual partner later. It is usually the case that such imprinting must occur in the first few days of life if it is to occur at all – another example of a sensitive period.

Educationists have taken this concept and applied it to human learning. There are several reasons why this may be undesirable.

In the first place, some of the 'facts' may be untrue. For instance, imprinting is not as irreversible as Lorenz thought, nor is the sensitive period so clear cut. Using appropriate techniques, children can be taught to read long before they are 'ready' (although it is not necessarily good for them), and on the other hand people can learn language for the first time quite late in life. The report (p. 12) says that babies expect cuddling during an early critical period, but Schaffer and Emerson (1964) have shown that quite a few babies do not. Secondly, some of the facts may have other explanations; for instance, it is possible that dogs reared in deprived environments suffer traumatic shock when they are faced with the 'real' world. But probably the most important criticism is that if one says that phenomena are due to sensitive periods one usually stops investigating further. The concept of sensitive learning periods has a connotation of maturation and decay, but it is likely that very few of the so-called senstitive periods are simply maturational phenomena. There are probably many reasons for the appearance of such periods. Some of them are given below.

Onset. This period may be determined by:

a. Maturation of the nervous or endocrine systems.

b. A child having reached the appropriate stage of cognitive development. For instance, Piaget has discovered a series of stages in the child's understanding and ability to solve problems. If stage C has not been reached, it will be impossible to go on to D.

c. 'Positive transfer'. Many kinds of learning depend

on previous learning. A child cannot learn to read, for instance, if he has not learned to discriminate shapes.

Offset. This period may be determined by:

a. Atrophy and decay.

b. Competition 'negative transfer' from habits already learned. For instance, a chimpanzee reared in the dark, or a blind person operated on for congenital cataract, will have learned to adapt to the environment using other senses than vision. When vision is restored, the learning which already exists may prevent or retard new learning. Similarly, habits of pronunciation make it more difficult for older people to learn to speak a foreign language.

c. A possible change in motivation. A bird may stop following moving objects because the fear of movement develops later than the tendency to follow, and finally overcomes it. An infant's fear of strangers develops in the second half of the first year of life, and overcomes the tendency to smile at faces.

d. A change of interests. Although a child may still be motivated by curiosity, he will be curious about a different set of things as he grows older.

There is no doubt that the concept of sensitive learning periods has served a useful function in drawing attention to phenomena which might otherwise have been missed. In particular, since many of these periods occur early in life, the concept has once more drawn attention to the potency of early learning. However, the term should be used with caution, and since the periods are often not clear-cut, a term such as 'optimal learning period' is preferable.

Finally, when such a period is identified, one should not be content to label it. Further investigation may show the reasons for its existence, and show ways of modifying it when necessary.

Language

The Report (p. 19) rightly supports the view that 'language ... is central to the educational process', but in doing this it gives the impression, at least to this reader, that language is essential for all intellectual development. Perhaps it is useful to draw attention to the work of Furth (1966) who has shown, with large numbers of deaf children and adults, that many advanced forms of thinking may show little or no impairment even though the thinker has a minute vocabulary and minimal syntax. There is also little positive evidence (see Carroll (1964) for a summary) for the Whorfian hypothesis, that there are differences in thinking between people with different first languages. Also adults with brain injury which results in language impairment are usually able to solve quite complex problems. One might even be able to make a case for saying that the language one uses for communicating (including jargon) may impair some kinds of thinking.

The case for making language central to education is to aid communication between people from different backgrounds, and to give children an optimal chance of enjoying and taking part in the verbal arts. Of course, we emphasize language too because most of our teaching and testing is done verbally.

Play and discovery

In several places (e.g. pp. 193 and 201) the Report emphasizes the importance of play and the value of 'discovery' methods. The authors may be right, but it should be pointed out that there is little evidence regarding what the importance and value are. Most children play, and most of the time they are playing they appear to be pre-occupied, and often happy, which is rewarding for the teacher. However, it is impossible to find out experimentally what would happen to a child who is not allowed to play. Experiments with monkeys are possible, and according to the Harlows (1962) if young monkeys are prevented from social play with other monkeys, the consequences may be disastrous for the later sexual behaviour of the animal. If one could extrapolate to humans, it would be necessary to emphasize that play should be social – at least at certain ages.

There are many kinds of discovery methods, which rely on a child's curiosity and apparent drive to control his environment. (Even some extreme 'environmentalists' among academic psychologists now admit the existence of exploratory or curiosity drives.) What is not known is what aspects of the environment are best learnt through discovery, and whether the results are due simply to improved motivation. If this were the case, then one would need to know if this motivation gets satiated. Does a child have a limited amount of 'discovery drive'? It is possible, in a rather gross way, to evaluate discovery methods, though the difficulties of evaluation of educational methods are great, and it is often unwise to generalize the results. In one survey of such studies, Ausubel (1961) concludes that there is no good evidence that children learn better through discovery methods. In one study of older children learning arithmetical principles (Kersh, 1962) the experimenter was obviously dismayed to find that rote learning was superior to directed discovery. Of course, in many of these evaluative studies, only short term cognitive gain has been investigated, and not longer term effects, or changes in attitude, etc. However, the moral is quite clear – that in deciding between educational methods, intuition is not enough.

Learning theory

For a student beginning to learn psychology, the classification of theorists in the Report (p. 192) is misleading. 'Learning theories' are concerned with learning which has very little to do with classroom learning. Psychologists use the word learning to describe the process by which any behaviour is modified, more or less permanently, as a result of experience. The term is applied to the behaviour of lower animals, to changes in human emotional expression and pulse rate, to the acquisition of sensory-motor skills. In this sense of the word, a child learns not to wet the bed, learns to be afraid of school, learns to be anti-social. One may well object that this is a gross misuse of the word, but this is how psychologists use it, and the point must be made clearly if 'learning theory' is being described. There are indeed two main kinds of learning theory, but not those described in the report.

One kind uses a more cognitive approach, and derives historically from the work of Köhler and other *gestalt* psychologists. The key concept is, perhaps, 'insight'. The other kind derives from Pavlov and Thorndike, and places emphasis on the learning of stimulus-response connexions, and on the concept of 'reinforcement'.

Piaget is not basically classed as a learning theorist. Unfortunately he says very little about the learning process. Learning is said to occur through the processes of assimilation and accommodation. Perhaps it does, but the teacher does not get much practical help from this discovery. The progress of the child is said to depend on his active learning in an appropriate environment, which makes intuitive sense, but requires analysis and particularizing. Piaget's enormous contribution has not been on

49

the understanding of learning, but in demonstrating how a child's *thinking* differs from that of an intelligent adult, and how the child shows changes in *capacity* for solving problems needing certain concepts.

The learning theories were developed mainly from animal work, and they have some application in understanding not classroom learning so much as the way a child behaves or conducts himself. Pavlov helps one understand how a child may develop a phobia for arithmetic, but is not much help in understanding how the child learns arithmetic once he has recovered from the phobia. In the writer's view, classical conditioning (Pavlov) is a useful model to describe changes in a child's motivation and emotion. Operant conditioning (B. F. Skinner) provides a useful model for describing changes in a child's outward behaviour. The work on operant conditioning is particularly important for teachers since there are now many demonstrations of the extent to which a child's behaviour is controlled by 'reinforcers' from the environment. Many of these reinforcers are directly under a teacher's control, and there are at present a large number of experiments being carried out in the classroom using these techniques.

Children also learn by imitation. The Freudian concept of 'identification' gives understanding of some of the processes, but more useful to the teacher is some of the empirical work, for instance by Bandura and his colleagues (Bandura and Walters, 1963), who have demonstrated the extent to which chidren copy from adults and from television, especially aggressive actions.

The acquisition of attitudes, beliefs, values and tastes seems to occur largely as a function of imitation or identification. As the Report points out, for pre-school children the model usually comes from the family circle, but for adolescents (and increasingly for pre-adolescents) the major influences seem to be peer-groups and mass media. There is some evidence that fictional (including television) heroes are particularly important for pre-adolescent boys. The cross-cultural evidence is so emphatic on the cultural and sub-cultural influences on children in these age groups that one wonders at the relative lack of emphasis given in the Report.

Classroom learning, in the layman's sense, can be categorized in several ways, but for psychological purposes the following is useful.

The learning of techniques and skills. The earliest skills include locomotion, feeding oneself, putting on one's clothes; then come skills required for communication such as speaking and listening, reading and writing. Children are also required to learn techniques of computing. At the other end of the age range are skills concerned with vocational training. Also in school, children are taught other skills and techniques in connexion with artistic creation and performance, and sports. A similar psychological analysis applies to all of these and perhaps also to social skills. One of the best ways of looking at the situation is to think of the skill or technique as being hierarchically structured. At the bottom of the structure are what have been called lower order habits which are necessary if the skill as a whole is to develop. For instance, before a child can write, he must have habits concerned with grasping a pencil, pressing it the right amount when moving across paper, drawing closed circles and lines at various orientations and so on. This hierarchical structure determines to a large extent the order in which habits should be taught. Also relevant to the analysis are concepts such as feed-back, massed and spaced practice, and the desirability of responding actively for efficient learning.

The learning of supposed facts, names for things, and

classifications. Here the experimental work has shown up the importance of repetition, and of a frame of reference in which to organize the material. Most of the relevant work has been done under the heading of memory rather than learning. This is probably because some of the most interesting work on memory has been done with verbal material, whereas most of the experimental work on learning has been done with non-verbal material.

Of particular relevance is the work of Bartlett who demonstrated among other things, the selective and distorting effects which a person's interests have on his remembering. The changing interests of a child as he grows older effect not only what he will learn but in what form he remembers it.

The acquisition of concepts and methods of solving problems. Piaget has described the changes in the child's capacity for doing this. The conditions which are best for the child's development are not clear, but many psychologists are now investigating the subject (for instance Bruner, Olver and Greenfield, 1966). What is clear is that children differ widely in their strategies of solving problems.

Learning to follow rules and to be original. 'Following rules' describes much of what a child does in applying principles, techniques and so on (once he has learned them) but very little is known psychologically about the processes involved. Usually the rules embody verbal or other symbolic guides regarding operations and the sequence in which they are to be performed (for instance in playing music, and in reading). The learner must be able to decode and encode, and keep to a correct temporal or spatial sequence. Many children can show this kind of behaviour at a very early age, before they are half-way through the Piagetian developmental stages.

There are ways of encouraging originality which most

teachers know about. There are also sophisticated methods such as Synectics (Gordon, 1961) which might or might not be appropriate in Junior Schools. The problem for the child is probably knowing how to discriminate between situations where originality is required (art) and where rule-following is advisable (choral singing and chemical formulae).

Learning to discriminate is involved in all of the more molar categories of learning mentioned above. For instance, in solving a problem, the solver must *discriminate* what kind of problem it is, and then follow the appropriate procedure. Failure in discrimination is a basic reason for many failures to learn at any age. The factors involved in discrimination learning are rather well understood and dealt with in most psychological textbooks.

Another process involved in all kinds of learning is transfer, which may be positive or negative, from previous to present learning. In many ways it is more helpful for a teacher to keep transfer in mind than to think of a child as passing through developmental stages. By doing this one thinks of readiness not so much in terms of maturation, but in terms of 'What has the child acquired already and has he the constituent skills, etc., which are necessary before passing on to his next task?' And considering along with this whether passing on would involve the child in undue stress for emotional or social reasons. In some cases of inability to learn, the problem is neither one of maturation nor negative transfer, but of some underlying disability. The disability may be of a gross kind, such as the excessive distractibility which sometimes goes with brain dysfunction, or specific as in certain kinds of dyslexia. Early diagnosis is highly desirable and, as Cotterell points out (1967) the age of nine mentioned in the Report (p. 214) is too late. Identifying specific disabilities requires skills which are ot taught to teachers of young children. They should be.

Conclusion

The psychology in the Report is disappointing in two main respects – its lack of emphasis on environmental effects, and on social motivational factors. By taking the view that the child 'must be allowed to develop' the authors emphasize the endogenous aspects of the child, about which the teacher can do nothing. Many children have a wretched home before coming to school, and have goals in life which teachers deplore. Along what lines should the child be allowed to develop? Luckily, when children come to school, their goals can still be modified, through reinforcement and through modelling on the behaviour of others. But at the top of the Primary age range, the modelling is likely to be on other children. The writer believes that at this age the major problems in education are caused by inappropriate rather than inadequate motivation. Bruner (1966) has edited a report of a conference on psychology concerned with education, particularly Primary education. It covers several areas of psychology which are very relevant to the subject of the Plowden Report. The reader is referred to a chapter by Kagan which presents briefly a useful analysis of the part played by motivation in a child's school learning. He concludes that, for every child who arrives at school with inappropriate goals, the 'teacher must salvage this child' before he can learn anything. For this to be possible, we need to try a variety of techniques and keep our minds open to different theoretical approaches.

4

Some Sociological Comments on Plowden

BASIL BERNSTEIN

Professor of Sociology of Education,
University of London Institute of Education

BRIAN DAVIES

Lecturer in Sociology of Education,
University of London Institute of Education

Introduction

Now that the once fashionable pastime of 'waiting for Plowden' has given way to the rapidly institutionalized sport of baiting it, it may well be most useful to ask first, in general terms, what sort of critique of its content is liable to prove most useful. Given the breadth of the Council's terms of reference – to enquire into 'primary education in all its aspects' (Plowden, 1967, Vol. 1, p. 1) – what can reasonably be expected of the Report is that firstly, it should recognize the social dimensions of its problems, secondly, that it should recognize existing work already in the field and thirdly, that it should exhibit a willingness to look at evidence without implicit preference for certain forms of explanation over others. The Report, like previous reports of the Central Advisory Council, sets out to encompass descriptively a huge field of practice in schools. On the strength of its findings, arrived at in the light of current evidence, it recommends numerous changes. The twin necessities of describing and recommending without offending seem to have induced in the Report a lack of analytic rigour not conducive to good sociological explanation, the essential character of which is to 'look behind' the publicly acknowledged reasons for our arrangements (see Berger, 1966, Burns, 1967). To be quite explicit, the Report, as Peters and others in this volume are ready to point out, regularly leaps from value to fact in respect of all of its central themes. It can be shown to be committed to a particular horiticultural view of child nature and development (Plowden, 1967, Vol. 1, Part II passim) and to a particular view of the teacher, school and curriculum which this committment logically entails. In general terms, this view comes very close to the semi-official ideology of primary education in this country, the most systematic exposition of which may be found in many colleges of education. Even if the manifest intentions for reform in Plowden come to nothing, therefore, its possible latent function as official reinforcement (better still, *martyred* official reinforcement) for such views must be brought out and the views exposed to examination.

A constructive sociological critique will, then, have two sides to it. It will look at any explicit models of the child, home, school, teacher or curriculum in the Report or make explicit those which are implicit. It will also examine what the Report does with existing sociological evidence and the light shed by its own evidence. The Report acknowledges that divisions in description and analysis of the various facets of primary education are somewhat inconvenient. For the sake of brevity and coherence we shall nevertheless look at the child, homes and parents, teachers and schools in sequence. This paper is not so much a critique of Plowden, but rather an attempt to add a sociological perspective to the discussion of pupils, teachers and the primary school.

The child

The model of the child in the Report is essentially biological. The child's growth is regarded as best viewed as
passing through a series of stages behaviourally, intellec-
tually and emotionally. The child's successive problems
and ultimate maturity are presented as basically developmental. There is an implicit but marked playing down
of age and age-grouping as sources of identity and interests (Plowden, 1967, Vol. 1, p. 10, para. 20). The over-
whelming characteristic of children insisted upon in
chapters one and two is their individual difference. Childhood is seen essentially as a series of ends in itself, change
within it from one phase to another being marked by
critical periods of maximum learning – sensitivity and
readiness. The existence of such periods is demonstrated
by examples from animal psychology and ethology. They
are assumed to be the case for humans, despite the statement that 'we do not know to what extent such periods
occur in the development of children' (Para. 28). There is
a tendency to equate the development of behaviour with
the development of cognitive behaviour (Paras. 42-52) to
which the growth of language is seen as vital (Para. 54).
The views of Piaget and Inhelder are quoted in respect of
cognitive and Luria and Bernstein in respect of linguistic
development. Emotional developments, like the intellectual, 'follow a regular sequence' (Para. 65), while social
development moves crucially through stages (Para. 72).
In all of these respects, development is viewed as the
product of an interaction of nature and nurture, with a
possibility of the environment being inadequate, the child
becoming deprived and individual differences becoming
heightened. For example, lack of consistency in general
and early maternal absence in particular are noted as

important contributory factors capable of disturbing emotional development (Para. 70). Even more particularly, going to school for the first time may lead to a major crisis for the child in respect of emotional and learning difficulties if mother encourages over-dependency at this time (Para. 71).

In general, this is a view of 'the child' from one perspective. 'Stages' figure in explanation to the exclusion of sub-cultural differences. There is a lack of a sufficient grasp of the varieties in family background. How such variation can lead to different degrees of preparedness of the child is not systematically brought out, despite the evidence of the surveys. A notion of the very different orders of role relationships into which children may be socialized before school-going, would give a much wider perspective on the potential significance of that event. Apart from a brief observation in chapter ten, upon the propriety of parents having some say in the 'readiness' of their child for school, the Report has nothing to say, other than that which is noted above, on the matter. While systematic research in this field is relatively recent, it is known that different children arrive at school with thoroughly different initial orientations toward it and their role as pupil: that they come with differential capabilities for role-playing and for meeting the requirements of the school situation. The tendency to espouse an 'undifferentiated' view of the child at school-going age is not Plowden's alone. (See Parsons, 1961.) These differences arise, not so much from a biological basis or relatively unique psychological characteristics of parents, but from differences in the social background of families which are related in turn to differences in language use, values and forms of social control.

Work has been done in recent years by the London Institute of Education Sociological Research Unit upon a

range of issues bearing upon the relationship between
the home and the primary school. The pre-school child
is largely dependent for his ideas of the school on what
his mother tells him about it or how she interprets the
experience of his brothers and sisters to him. Evidence
suggests a strong relationship between social class and the
extent of the mother's preparation of her child for school.
In a total sample of over three hundred familes, working-
class mothers have been shown to make minimal preparation, while nearly half of the middle-class mothers mention three or more ways in which they prepare the child.
(To be published in a future Sociological Research Unit
Monograph by Routledge & Kegan Paul). Bernstein has
drawn attention to the importance of the differential
awareness of mothers to the educational functions of
play and toys and suggests that

> Working-class children often have to learn at school what
> is part of the experience of the middle-class child. *Some*
> middle-class mothers understand, even if they do not
> always approve, the classroom world of the infant school.
> Many working-class mothers are at a loss to see what it all
> means. For a child of these mothers, school is one thing
> and his life outside school a very different thing. For
> many middle-class children, the home and the school are
> in step; for working-class children this is *not* the case.
> This continuity and discontinuity affects the extent
> to which the child can benefit from school and
> benefit cannot be measured only by grades and examina-
> tions (Bernstein 1967).

Many children from both middle- and working-class backgrounds are, in different ways, inadequately prepared for
school.

Plowden also ignores the cultural shaping and expression of biological sex-differences, an omission which may

again be related to its narrowly psychologistic view of the child. On this particular point, Blyth notes that the cultural expression of sex-differences in behaviour in middle childhood cut across class differences, while he suggests that peer group relationships exhibit interesting differences between classes. In general, he suggests 'that the cultural component in the characteristic behaviour of children in the middle years is much greater than has often been realized' (Blyth, 1965, Vol. II, pp. 11-12), and in this respect, his strictures upon the 1931 Report (pp. 4, 5) may be extended to include Plowden.

It is this sort of failure to get clear the social significance of age that leads the Report to an inconsistent stand upon the relationship between developmental and chronological age and their bearing upon the ages of transfer. Despite the vital importance attached to developmental age (Para. 75), the Report concludes that children are better with friends in their own age-group unless there is clear evidence to the contrary. The sort of 'clear evidence' that is seen as potentially admissible might relate, for instance, to the advisibility of transferring early maturing girls from the top of the middle school before the normal age of transfer (Para. 377). At a more general level, the new suggested ages of transfer from first and middle schools, at eight and twelve respectively, are justified in terms of a number of criteria of a developmental and cognitive order. On a particular issue of age-mixing, the Report fails to decide upon the advisibility of vertical (or 'family') groupings in the infants school (Paras. 799-804). It does come down quite firmly in favour, though, of separate first and middle schools on pedagogic grounds (Para. 426).

What is never really made clear is any recognition of the positive importance of age-status to young children.

In changing the ages of entering and leaving schools, the Report is in fact redefining the notion of childhood.

Blyth, who was aware that Plowden was considering this matter when he produced his study, points out some of the possible effects of such a change for both children and schools. For example, at the top end of the middle school, he believes that the change proposed may 'have the effect of reducing the girl's predominance in the good pupil role' (op cit. p. 189). As referred to above, the Report is willing to see some of this same category of girls singled out for early promotion to secondary education. Yet this willingness to countenance extreme variability in the treatment of children has to be contrasted with the rigid notion adopted by the Report upon the need for separate first and middle schools. The unacknowledged reason for their proposed separateness could be adjudged more important than those officially avowed. That is to say, that 'children, like adults, enjoy and are stimulated by novelty and change. The first day at school, the transfer to the "big school" are landmarks in the process of growing up.' Children hang on to 'the myth that "going up" must mean going to something better' (Para. 427). In other words, that passing from one important age-category to another is both eased and stamped-in by the ritual of changing school, by the physical removal of the child from the context of his old status to that of the new.

In broad terms, the Report would have enabled us to see much more clearly the inter-relationships between the biological and cultural components of childhood if it had examined the recent changes which have taken place in the structure of the family and processes of socialization. It is a loss that it did not discern the importance of this sort of analysis from Crowther, which placed the development of the education of 15-18 year-old pupils in the perspective of relevant social, economic and demographic changes.

Homes and Parents

It is held as an important truth in the Report that 'the child's physique, personality and capacity to learn develop as a result of a continuous interaction between his environmental and genetical inheritance' (Para. 75). Parents are thus important as providers of 'genetical inheritance' and of probably the most significant part of the child's environment. While genetic factors are unalterable, 'environmental factors are, or ought to be, largely within our control'.

From the whole orientation of the Report, it is clear that the assumption behind its views of homes and parents is that they can be altered and controlled. It is recognized that children grow up in different environmental backgrounds, in different socio-economic groups with their more or less 'adverse circumstances' providing conditions which affect body-size, the age of puberty, standards of nutrition, family size and intelligence (Paras. 33-38). However, although these facts are important for education 'in the light that they throw on progress, or lack of it, made towards equalizing even the simple circumstances of life between different classes', it is maintained that 'socio-economic classes are heterogeneous and artificial, and it is not so much the family's occupation or income that is operative here as its attitudes and traditions of child care, its child-centredness, its whole cultural outlook'. At the same time, 'the educational disadvantage of being born the child of an unskilled worker is both financial and psychological' (Para. 85).

It has been necessary to quote at length at this point in order to establish what the Report has to say in general terms about class differences. Let it be said immediately that any index of social class is bound to be relatively 'heterogeneous and artificial'. Nevertheless, the operational measures refer to real behaviour. Equally, let it be said that the terminological variability that attends the use of the concepts of 'class' and 'status' in sociology, and not least in respect of the sociology of education, may be calculated to confound even the well-meaning. At the same time, it is difficult not to believe that the Report systematically plays down the importance of social class in education. To conceive of it simply in terms of the Registrar General's occupational groupings is to conceive of it very narrowly. Such a view will tend to conceal differences acknowledged to be important for education. Even however in the Report's usage, there are differences revealed both by the 1964 National Survey reported and analysed in Volume 2, Appendices 3 to 7, and the Manchester Survey reported in Appendix 9, which would make it exceedingly difficult to ignore the importance of class both in respect of opportunity and educability. Evidence will be adduced below upon this point.

First of all, let us ask why class differences are treated in the Report in this way. One possible reason may be the seduction of a dual committment to the developmental view of the child described above and to a belief in egalitarianism (that social differences 'ought not' to exist) that makes psychological reductionism appealing. The more acceptable reason may be a lack of sociological insight at points of construction and interpretation of the Survey work. Regression analysis in the National Survey suggests the grouping of variables bearing upon children's progress in school into three categories representing (1) parental attitudes, (2) home circumstances, (3) schooling. The major conclusion reached as the result of the Survey is that 'variation in parental attitudes can account for more of the variation in children's school achievement than either the variation in home circumstances or the variation in schools'. Further, that there is no doubt that attitudes have changed and are changing (Plowden, 1967, Vol. 2, App. 4, p. 181, Para. 6). Moreover 'family size does not explain the children's test performances as effectively as the attitudes of their parents' (Plowden, 1967, Vol. I, Para. 90). On the question of 'whether the differences in circumstances account for the differences in attitudes ... (the) ... evidence ... suggests that parent's occupation, material circumstances and education explain only about a quarter of the variation in attitudes' (Para 100). Attitudes may therefore be alterable by persuasion.

Parental attitudes account in fact for 28 per cent of the variation in educational performance for all pupils between schools and for 20 per cent within schools. Thirty five per cent of the variation between schools and 54 per cent within schools is unaccounted for (Plowden, 1967, Vol. 1, p. 33, Table 1). The Manchester Survey in respect of both school and pupil analyses underlines the same factors, that 'economic level and social class are much less important than aspects of parental attitude' (Plowden, 1967, Vol. 2, App. 9, p. 381). Peaker, in his discussion of the National Survey, suggests that the inclusion of attitudes for the first time in such a survey adds a new dimension to the evidence of Crowther and Newsom (Plowden, 1967, Vol. 2, App. 4, p. 184, Para. 18). It necessarily leaves open, however, in terms of the Survey, speculation about the origins of the attitudes which parents exhibit. No one would wish to espouse a deterministic argument concerning the relationship between socio-economic status and attitudes to education. But one would wish to guard against an argument that avoided including attitudes as a dimension of class differences. It would be as well to look very closely at this vital question of their relationship in the National Survey.

The total sample of parents taken as the basis for the survey shows some discrepancy from the Registrar General's percentage figures given for the married male population aged 20-64 (Plowden, 1967, Vol. 2, App. 3, p. 100, Para. 2, 3). More important than this, the argument advanced that the connection between home circumstances, parental attitudes and children's achievement 'is analogous to the relations between the statuses of fathers, mothers and children' (App. 4, p. 184, Para. 18), involves a rather misleading depiction of factor analysis. The 'mother' and 'father' of children's achievement, that is to say, parental attitudes and home circumstances, are constructs rather than givens. Concretely, one is inclined to quarrel with the treatment of variables such as whether parents have taken any recreational or leisure courses, whether the family goes on outings together, and even more strongly, literacy of the home and elements of the category of parental interest and support as attitudinal factors. (See the classifications of variables into factor groupings in Vol. 2, App. 4, Table 1.) The criterion for allocating these variables appears to have become confused with a notion of their being 'less firmly anchored in the past' than are variables like parent's occupation and education which are classified under home circumstances (App. 4, p. 183, Para. 11). To take one quite specific example, membership of a public library, taken as a component of literacy of the home and classed as an attitude factor in the Survey, shows class differences significant at more than the .001 level for both mothers and children in research undertaken by the Institute's Sociological Research Unit (see p. 59, line 12).

In other words, whereas social class is defined relatively unambiguously in terms of father's occupation, there is no clear definition of 'attitude'. It covers statements of fact, intention and disposition. On the basis of some rather inexplicit criterion of 'immediacy', important factors like the literacy of the home and paternal interest shown in the Survey and by other work (and further examined below) to be strongly linked to social class, have been arbitrarily assigned to the attitudinal factor in the regression analysis. To do this is to divorce class in an indefensible way from its behavioural concomitants.

That class (in the sense of the Registrar General's groups) is systematically related to educational factors is not in any sense denied in the Survey work; it is merely systematically played down, particularly in the Report. In the summary of some of the interrelations between parental attitudes to education, home circumstances and class, there is a uniform gradient from Class I to V in respect of differences in responsibility and initiative taken by parents over the child's education, paternal interest and support, knowledge of work that the child was doing and the literacy of the home (Plowden, 1967, Vol. 2, App. 3, p. 147, Table 67). The strongest class gradients on the item clusters in fact appear in respect of paternal interest and literacy of the home. While these obviously imply attitudes, what they essentially refer to is the role system of the family and the range and quality of the communication it is transmitting. They reflect conceptions of how members of the family understand their rights and obligations rather than attitudes readily susceptible to change.

The Survey evidence concerning the role of the father in respect of the child's education is left particularly in mid-air. The National Survey established information about paternal attitudes and characteristics (as on all other aspects of parental attitudes) via the administration of a structured questionnaire by Social Survey Interviewers to mothers. It is important to be explicit upon this point; the data that we have upon the paternal role is essentially the opinion of wives delivered to what may in many cases, have been perceived as officialdom. The evidence gathered reveals strong social class gradients in respect of both husband's interest in the choice of school that the child went to and as to whether the husband had talked to the head of the child's school. The difference is less marked between classes in respect of father's interest in the child's progress with 68 per cent even of Class V fathers reported as taking an interest (Plowden, 1967, Vol. 2, App. 3, p. 118, Table 21). The average score on the item cluster 'paternal interest and support' shows the general class trend (App. 3, p. 147, Table 67). On the less specifically educational question, however, of whether the husband took a big part in controlling the children, responses for groups I to V are, in fact, uniformly high and show no significant trend (App. 3, p. 118, Table 21). On the evidence given, it is clear that, generally, responsibility for the child's education becomes more exclusively maternal as the class scale is descended.

It would seem that many working-class fathers do not support and develop the educational role of their children. It may well be that as a result, the working-class boy does not come to value his educational role as this is not identified with his most significant male relation. The father may point here to the occupational role without it being connected to the educational role. This situation may well be reinforced by the almost totally feminine world of the infant school. It would not be surprising, therefore to find girls over-represented increasingly down the class scale, for these sorts of reasons, in 'good pupil' success roles, and boys similarly under-represented. Plowden does not present evidence broken down by age, sex and socio-economic category, which would allow such a view to be tested. In Volume 1, the discernible references to sex difference amount, in fact, to noting differences in physical rates of maturation, 'the poorer resilience of boys than girls under adverse circumstances' (Plowden, 1967, Vol. 1, p. 7) and that the games that girls and boys tend to play at the top of the Junior School are different (p. 258, Para. 708).

There are equally striking class gradients exhibited over differences between the type of school parents hoped that their child (when in the final junior year) would go to and the type that the child was in fact going to (Vol. 2, App. 3, p. 122, Table 28. The interview of parents took place at the end of the school year when the 11 + results were known.); or again, as to 'whether any type of secondary was particularly disliked' (Vol. 2, App. 3, p. 123, Table 32); in terms of parent's preferences for streaming by ability (App. 3, p. 142, Table 60); or as to 'other things' which worried parents, indicating that parents highest up in the class scale worry most about things like size of school class. Deprivation is indeed a relative thing (App. 3, p. 144, Table 65). Factors which might count in interpreting these differences probably relate to a whole range of variables. Particularly highlighted are differences in parent's objective knowledge of the situation in schools, in their relative feelings of power or ineffectiveness in respect of school and their ability to express those feelings. It is particularly difficult to understand the failure in the Report to connect up the finding of the National Survey (App. 3, p. 121, Table 27) in respect of parents attitudes toward their children 'staying on' with the suggested importance by the Manchester Study of preferred age of leaving as the best single indicator of favourable parental attitudes and hence attainment for the average or backward child (App. 9, p. 382, Para. 109).

It may be as well to repeat that one is not attempting to deny the importance of parental attitudes for the child's educational attainment. Rather, one is suggesting that to underestimate the social principles which are responsible for the shaping of attitudes may make the problem of their change more difficult. The Report, although hopeful that these attitudes may be favourably manipulated, has virtually no positive evidence to rely upon. Peaker points out that 'such evidence as we have on this point is not very encouraging'. (Vol. 2, App. 4, p. 181). (The little encouragement available is reported in Vol. 1, p. 43, Paras. 113-117. The limited evidence given appears open to several interpretations. As a striking example of the danger of the self-fulfilling prophecy in sociology, see Hornsby-Smith, M.P., 1968. More importantly, the findings of Young and McGeeny, 1968, signally fail to clarify this area. Particular attention should be paid to their presentation and discussion of test-score evidence between pp. 91-95. There are two sorts of considerations that appear to be important here. In the first place, it must be borne in mind that the relationship established between parental interest and school attainment is correlational rather than causal. In other words, the Report tends to suggest that greater parental interest leads positively to improved attainment. It is, of course, possible that the link in some instances runs the other way; that good attainment by the child leads to increasing parental interest.

One must assume that the link is at least partly reciprocal. Links between small family size and relatively high education aspiration for children must be thought of in the same way. If this is a possibility, then the attempt to 'generate' interest on the part of schools among parents by means described in Chapter 4, may prove a great deal more difficult than is envisaged in the Report or in much subsequent comment (see Blackstone, 1967, p. 300). Moreover, such interest if produced may be more transient than the 'spontaneous' sort.

The second consideration relates to how clear we can be about the proper relationship of the parent to the school. The Report is not without its difficulties in this matter. We shall see presently that its attitude toward Parent-Teacher Associations is ambivalent. This is merely one aspect of the complex of issues relating to parent's actual knowledge of school matters, the desirable extent of that knowledge from the school's point of view and the use to which increased knowledge may be put by parents. It is clear that many parents simply do not know enough about school and that the tendency for this to be the case increases with occupational descent. The Report acknowledges this in several places (Plowden, 1967, Vol. 1, Paras 102-106). What it fails to see is that among parents whose objective knowledge of school affairs is extensive, pressures to achieve may be equally (though more insidiously) hurtful to the child. In the general sense, the development of modern methods, particularly in the Infant School, has probably made it more difficult for parents to co-operate in an active capacity in their child's education. Current pedagogy, with its requirement of specialized teaching techniques which are difficult for the parent to learn, may have led to a greater exclusion of the working-class parent from the child's school experience. If this is the case, then it will be positively dangerous to raise the aspirations of parents unless schools can work out a genuinely meaningful area of shared concern. If this can in fact be done, then it may help to remove the wedge which exists in certain cases between the role of child and that of pupil – another less palatable fact concerning the existing discontinuity between home and school, of which the Report remains largely unaware.

In conclusion of this section, it is possible to agree strongly with the Manchester study's descriptive comment upon the importance of parental interest as a factor in children's brightness which suggests that 'the situation might not be quite as simple as it looks' (Plowden, 1967, Vol. 2, App. 9, p. 382, Para. 110). The whole picture presented in the Report of the attitudes which are taken to lie behind and regulate that interest in parents is blurred. Moreover, the conception of 'the child' presented tends to overshadow the cultural and social shaping of the roles of children of different sexes from differing class backgrounds. The situation insofar as they both bear upon children's school progress is indeed more heterogeneous than Plowden discerns.

Schools

Social aspects of school organization are relatively neglected in Plowden. The implicit picture that one comes away with from its pages is of children in the majority of schools happily progressing in self-regulating groups. As a picture, this is deceptively superficial. At the general level, although the Report talks explicitly about aims and purposes in education, it fails to distinguish these from 'functions' in the social sense. A link between schools and society is acknowledged, couched in the sort of inexplicit terms which only Crowther (Crowther, 1959, Vol. 1, Ch. 5) among Central Advisory Council reports on schools managed to surmount. In Plowden, schools have the task of preparing children to fit into a society which is rapidly changing, becoming more affluent and which will demand flexible though balanced people (Plowden, 1967, Vol. 1, p. 185). The difficulty of reaching statements upon aims (used in the sense of consensus as to goals to be pursued) is acknowledged, although a statement of goals whose acceptance and pursuit represents 'a general and quickening trend' is offered as a check-list (p. 187,

Para. 502). One such goal which schools pursue is the attempt 'to equalize opportunities and to compensate for handicaps' (Para. 505). The normative intention of this and the whole paragraph in which it is embedded, despite its misleading opening, is clear. Education does offer an increasingly important avenue of social mobility and probably does on balance lessen overall deficiencies in life-chances. Unless, however, the meaning of 'compensate for handicaps' is made much more explicit and the social organization of the school is observed in terms of how it perpetuates such handicaps, we have few clear guides to amelioration. In wider terms, the section on goals in the Report falls short of an objective appraisal of the social functions of primary education. (For a view of the U.S. elementary school see Parsons, 1961. For a specific discussion of the functions of the English primary school see Blyth, W. A. L., op cit., Vol. 1, although the discussion is marred by a peculiar use of terminology. For a wider discussion that fails to avoid a shading off from the emphirical to the normative, see Goslin, 1965.)

The only general attempt to describe schools is contained in the evaluation of all primary schools by H.M.I.S. who suggest a classificatory scheme of nine intuitive, hazy categories (Plowden, 1967, Vol. 1, p. 100, Para. 267 seq). This is supplemented by the description of three good, 'composite' schools. The whole section is closed by the suggestion that 'what goes on in primary schools cannot greatly differ from one school to another, since there is only a limited range of material within the capacity of primary school children' (Para. 289), a comment which epitomizes the triviality of this whole area of the Report.

Streaming is virtually the only aspect of school organization (barring the study of management reported in Appendix 13) given detailed consideration. The Report on balance rejects streaming (Para. 833). The N.F.E.R. study on the effects of streaming in junior schools (Appendix 11), which is the preliminary report of a fuller work due for publication this year, would not of itself sustain this conclusion. It offers only the judgement 'that the question – to stream or not to stream? – reveals itself as the research continues – to require a far more complex and nuanced answer than the propagandists on both sides would have one believe' (Plowden, 1967, Vol. 2, App. 11, p. 555, Para. 1.2). What the research reported does tend to suggest is that teachers' attitudes, values and practices are more significant than the form of school organization. This will be commented upon below. Without offering any social class data, the Report accepts that the research shows 'some evidence which suggests that achievement in the limited field of measurable attainment is higher in streamed schools. It is not so marked as to be decisive' and as 'organization can reflect and reinforce attitudes', those schools 'which treat children individually will accept unstreaming throughout' (Plowden, 1967, Vol. 1, p. 291, Paras 818-9). The survey itself points out that the tests of attainment used may tend to favour children in streaming schools subject to more traditional forms of curricula and teaching and fail to record abilities which unstreamed schools may foster (Plowden, 1967, Vol. 2, App. II, p. 574, Para. 3.1).

There is a wider issue here which the Report does in fact discern, although it is not clear whether it sees all of its implications. It is felt that schools should work out their own tests for children (Plowden, 1967, Vol. 1, p. 201, Para. 551) and that authorities who retain interim secondary selection should cease to rely upon external tests (p. 471). At the same time, it is recommended that 'there should be recurring national surveys of attainment' (p. 473). The wide issue at stake is the question of the sort

SOME SOCIOLOGICAL COMMENTS ON PLOWDEN

of attainment that primary schools are working to in the
first place. How are standards to be defined in the 'discovery' ethos proposed? What are their relationships
to the teacher's classroom objectives? And what sort of
testing procedures are appropriate to attainments which
result from the school processes envisaged? From the
point of view of the teacher, the answers to these questions are of vital importance.

In the same sort of context, the urge to achieve con-
tinuity between stages in education leads to the suggestion that 'there should be a detailed folder on each child
which could provide a basis for a regular review with
children's parents of their progress' (p. 471). The details
of what the folder should contain are fully specified (pp.
161-2). The organizational imperatives of the 11 + are to
be replaced by individualized rule by dossier. It is interesting to speculate upon the possible mechanics and
consequences of keeping such folders. There would be
questions of who wrote them up and controlled them;
the problem of the evaluative categories to be used in
them; difficulties of confidentiality and access. None of
these problems are considered in the Report. (For a notion
of some of the problems that might arise in this respect,
albeit discussed in the context of the U.S. high-school,
see Cicourel, A. V. and Kitsuse, J. I., 1963.)

The question of 'who decides what?' in schools is also
generally neglected. There is no systematic exposition of
the role of either the head or assistant teacher. It is
strongly argued that schools need to be permeable to
parents and a very large number of devices are discussed
in Chapter 4 for improving their knowledge of and par-
ticipation in school processes. The argument stops short,
though, of universally endorsing Parent-Teacher Associations, despite members having been impressed by their
high quality 'as much as any aspect of education' in the

U.S.A. (Plowden, 1967, Vol. 1, p. 39, Para. 111) and the generally glowing examples of English P.T.A.s cited (paras. 107-110). The main reasons for this attitude are given as the danger of cliques of dominant parents arising, the failure of the lower-working class to participate, but most important, the danger that the head might not be able to give 'good leadership' or delegate P.T.A. running effectively (Para. 111). Given the positive fervour with which the Report espouses other methods of parent-participation, one suspects a capitulation here to professional dislike of the P.T.A. One surmises that behind that dislike lies a genuine difficulty of defining the legitimate boundaries of parent-teacher interests and competencies. Our primary schools have only recently begun to move away from being relatively 'closed' social institutions (our secondary schools in the main still are) and in all but a few cases, there is genuine lack of clarity about the boundaries and content of roles to be played by staff and parents toward one another. This is without doubt an area of great difficulty. Nevertheless, by failing to complement its other measures for parental-participation with a more positive affirmation of P.T.A. work, Plowden is risking the build-up without the pay-off. It is also failing to recognize the different nature of the boundaries and contents of the roles of parents from varying social class backgrounds vis-a-vis the school. It merely accepts in this respect the importance of 'habit' in schools and the particular risk that innovation tends to run aground amid the conservatism of teachers (p. 187, Para. 503). It is nonetheless prepared to run the risk of upsetting habits in respect of punishment (p. 269, Para. 743 seq.). In both of these cases, the situation begs for at least a recommendation to further research on the extent and function of habit, stereotypes and ideology in schools, especially as they bear upon resistance and change. There is not even

F

a hint that those teachers in school who are recognized as having to lean habitually upon coercion may not instantly accept the new forms of control implicit in the superior types of pupil-teacher relationships envisaged in the Report. Or that they may still be inclined, with physical coercion ruled out, even as a last resort, to lean on measures designed to produce psychic pain which may be equally or more undesirable than that induced by corporal punishment.

That there are limits to parents' rights in general in primary schools is a position parallelled in the Report by its proposal in respect of nursery schools to limit children's entry. Here where mothers 'cannot satisfy the authorities that they have exceptionally good reasons for working', the entry of their children is to be given low priority (p. 469). There might be considerable difficulty in rendering this administratively possible without great arbitrariness of definition. The Report believes it proper, in fact, to wash its hands of responsibility for the dangers of the 'alternative arrangements' that it knows in some cases will be made (p. 127, Para. 330).

At the same time, the Report's notions upon educational priority areas and the need for positive discrimination toward them go in the right direction and the slogans are probably necessary spurs to public policy. The suggestion of a 'sustained effort ... to diversity the social composition' of these districts happily amounts to no more than a desire to provide houses for teachers (p. 67). The areas are to be defined in terms of a battery of criteria (pp. 57-9). In general, they will be marked as places where children are most severely handicapped by home conditions. The areas are viewed as needing more teachers, aides, money, college links and teachers' centres. They should see the first developments in social work and community schools. The vital consideration of deciding why some of the schools in these areas *do* in fact work, and building upon this knowledge rather than shunting in extra resources willy-nilly, is in fact recognized as a priority for further research (p. 426, Para 1165 (d)).

The community school as presently envisaged is merely a new name for play centres, youth clubs and evening institutes, with lip-service to Henry Morris, meeting on school premises (pp. 44-6). It is difficult to see them making any significant short-run contribution to education itself in the E.P.A.

There are relatively straight forward proposals which will bear upon schools which are well-conceived and ought to be welcomed. The introduction, for instance, of the single-term entry will provide a more satisfactory basis for the organization of the infant school. It will at the same time end the serious disadvantage of present arrangements to the summer-born child (p. 136), affirmed by numerous studies of streaming and attainment. Equally the call for a uniform, national policy on structure and transfer ages is both overdue and highly necessary in a country where even short-range geographic mobility by parents can transport a child to a completely different standard of provision. Such mobility is likely to increase and the disadvantage of changing schools ought not to be accentuated by gross variation in authority provision which has long been the scandal of the secondary sector.

The Curriculum

There is no justification for treating the curriculum apart from the school, nor indeed from considerations of pedagogy. A fully worked out sociology of the school would attempt to relate the nature of the beliefs and skills which are transmitted to the curriculum and pedagogy on the one hand and to the authorty relationships and organizational structure of the school on the other. The Report's view of the curriculum is inextricably linked to its view of child nature and the learning process. Its ideas upon child nature have been discussed above. Upon learning, it states that 'Piaget's explanations appear to most educationalists in this country to fit the observed facts of children's learning more satisfactorily than any other' (Plowden, 1967, Vol. 1, pp. 192-3). Play and interest are key aspects of the continuous process of learning. The rigid, subject-divided curriculum and timetable are rejected. In the free-day during which children take every opportunity to experience their environment, learning by discovery will take precedence over learning by description.

Essentially, the Report dichotomizes 'being told' and 'finding out' rather crudely. Its rationale is the pursuit of the long-term objective of living in and serving society being most probably achieved by happy adults who have lived fully as children (p. 188). The child lives most fully by finding out.

There are several far reaching implications of this position. For the teacher, it indicates quite specifically the role of arranger of context (discussed below). It crucially heightens the problem of the evaluation of children's progress and that of the pedagogy itself. It will serve to reduce the salience of traditional attainments in the evaluation of children. Pupil success will be defined less sharply in terms of the efficient recall of conventionally taught material. For certain sorts of children, there will be the necessity to learn specifically an unaccustomed 'play culture'.

The great bulk of curriculum information in the Report comes in Chapter 17, which is divided into 'traditional' subjects. Robert Dearden has dealt at length with the possible objections to the Council's views, particularly upon religious education. While there are almost Durkheimian echoes in some of the passages upon the school community and the Act of Worship, it may be held that the views expressed in these areas are platitudinous rather than prescriptive. One would argue that the infectious theory of value-transmission expressed in the belief 'that children will catch values and attitudes far more from what teachers do than what they say' (p. 312) is much nearer the heart of the Council's general notion of learning and the child than is its lapse into moral fervour.

Broadly then, the instrumental order of the primary school is envisaged as non-compartmentalized. Achievement will be thoroughly individualistic though not competitive. The expressive order is seen as informal and non-ritualized. Pupil-teacher relationships will tend to be friendly and therapeutic. Control measures will relate to individuals rather than to groups. Schools will be retively open and fluid institutions. This prospect is regarded by Plowden as wholly pleasing and few would disagree over it. However, it would be as well to acknowledge that the 'open' school will bring with it a different set of problems as well as its expected benefits.

Teachers

The school and curriculum envisaged will, it is repeatedly acknowledged, depend upon the teacher. At the risk of the accusation of waywardness, one would point out that in the forty-six plates which occupy virtually the whole of the chapter on 'Aids to Learning and Teaching', only two contain a teacher. One might be forgiven for imagining therefore that teachers are aids to neither. At least, the balance struck is consonant with the view, already noted, of the teacher as an arranger of context

or as a problem setter. This view springs from the premium placed upon 'readiness', which is a notion offered
for critical guidance in the teaching situation without
any evidence offered as to its signs or any systematic
answer to the question of 'for what?' The logical conclusion of this excessive commitment to individual differences can only be a one-to-one teaching relationship.

The hard fact is that even when questions of content
are answered, the signs of readiness are not always easily
seen. Especially in the context of the large infant school,
the teacher may sometimes confuse the inability of the
child to master a particular skill either with his lack of
interest or a failure on her part to present material in a
meaningful way. This is all part of the view that on no
account should the teacher impose anything upon the
child – 'until the child is ready to take a particular step
forward, it is a waste of time to teach him to take it'
(Plowden, 1967, Vol. 1, p. 25, para. 75). She must wait
until the child himself determines what should be made
available to him. Sin and virtue have changed sides in the
teaching transaction.

However, this latter possibility is swiftly corrected by
a positively Chaucerian picture of a typical classroom
situation where 'the teacher moved among individuals
and groups doing these and other things, and strove to
make sure that all were learning' (Para. 288). This teacher,
like any other, the Report explicitly points out, is responsible for the worthwhileness of what the children are
learning (Para. 553). However, it is impossible to discover
in the Report what this entails, unless implicitly that
what children learn is by definition worthwhile.

In the very short introduction to Part Six, we are told
that the role of the teacher is less crucial than was formerly thought, that the teacher is in some respect a
parent-substitute, that he must be nurturant yet capable

of evaluation in respect of the child, that he must have a highly individualistic approach to children's learning, that he must 'lead from behind' and perforce serve as a value-model. The teacher's role is 'bound to be at one and the same time satisfying and yet over-demanding'. 'The teacher's work can never be seen to be completed.' They run the danger of becoming child-like 'the more sensitive and conscientious (they) are' (pp. 311-12). This is once more a curious jumble of fact, myth and prescription but only more confused in degree than parts of the frequently quoted, short sociological analyses of the role (e.g., Wilson, 1962). There is nothing to be found in the Report upon teacher's career lines (not even comparable data on holding power of schools over staff, by areas, as provided by Newsom, 1963 Ch. 3, p. 23), upon the consequences of teaching for different lengths of time in different sorts of schools, typical success patterns in teaching or upon informal staff relationships and their possible differences by age, training or sex. We cannot therefore evaluate the effects of any of these things upon children. There is very little in the Report, other than in purely administrative terms, about the head teacher or the existing implications of the pattern of rewards in primary schools. One quite fascinating discovery in respect of Appendix I, 'A Questionnaire to Some Teachers', to which all replies are printed which 'have proved to be of interest', (Plowden, 1967, Vol. 2, App. I, p. 1, Para. 2), is that only two out of forty-one questions have been omitted. The first asks for opinions upon the basic salary scale, posts of responsibility and long service awards, the second asked whether men should be encouraged to teach infants (p. 11, Questions 28-9). It must be an exceedingly odd profession that fails to provide interesting opinions upon its own salary position or that fails to reflect upon this omission.

Contained in Plowden's view of the teacher there is an inexplicit assumption of role consensus, no questioning of how it is learned and no elaboration of its strains and satisfactions, of a systematic kind. One might have expected some reference to the way in which changes in science, maths and language teaching in the primary school is likely to strengthen the professional component of the role and perhaps weaken the stereo-type of the infant school teacher as a surrogate mother. The practical survey of teacher training, the urge to have it examined and the endorsement of the greater need for a variety of intakes of teachers to primary schools all appear good sense (Plowden, 1967, Vol. 1, Ch. 25). One suspects that research undertaken upon colleges of education and training departments will highlight a fundamental tension between the theoretical, liberal orientation of college staff and the more traditional orientation of teachers in practice schools in which students tend to get caught in a rather deadening and unproductive way.

Systematic information on one aspect of teachers is available in the research associated with the streaming study upon characteristics and attitudes exhibited in streamed and unstreamed schools (Plowden, 1967, Vol. 2, App. II, pp. 557-84). Exploratory research of fifty matched pairs of streamed and unstreamed schools by the N.F.E.R. led to the view that 'this difference in organization was reflected in, or arose from, very different views held by the teaching staff which in turn affected the choice of teaching methods' (p. 557). A complex piece of research which uses the rather unfortunate terms 'obsessive' and 'permissive' to dichotomise teaching characteristics, concludes that 'streamed and non-streamed schools embody different philosophies'; that although not all teachers conform to the predominant pattern of their school, 'the streamed school seems to be more systematic, concentrates more on conventional lessons, gives more attention to the 3-R's and is likely to be more traditional'. The non-streamed school has younger teachers 'who hold more permissive views on such things as manners, noise and cleanliness.... Their teaching tends to place more emphasis on self-expression, learning by discovery and practical experience' (p. 589). The survey offers no opinion upon the fascinating alternative posed above as 'reflected in, or arose from' but emphasizes that differences in streamed and unstreamed schools arise not only from organization but 'the whole climate of relationships built up by what teachers say and do and what they appear to their pupils to imply' (p. 573). The research hints at the importance of a whole nexus of relationships between values, recruitment, professional socialization and organizational arrangements and offers an insight to the possible sorts of built-in resistances to any change envisaged in schools. And yet this fails to be even mentioned in the areas for further studies in the body of the Report.

It may be thought that too much space has been devoted to negative criticism of the Report in these comments. This has not been the aim. There are a number of very positive features and recommendations within the body of the Report and these have been referred to by numerous commentators. All that has been attempted here is to try and show the type of questions which can be raised as a result of adopting a sociological standpoint.

5

The Positive Roles of Society and the Teacher

LIONEL ELVIN

Director, University of London Institute of Education

Introduction

The preceding papers have argued that the Plowden Report is inadequate in its thinking about each of the foundation subjects of educational study: the philosophy, the psychology and the sociology of the subject. The Report expounds an idea of education as a sort of natural growth, but without an analysis of the concept of 'nature' and with no recognition that we do not just grow but are encouraged to develop in one way rather than another by choices that parents, teachers and society make. From the point of view of the psychologist the Report is to be criticized because it does not distinguish between different kinds of learning, is naive in its explanations of play and 'discovery' in relation to learning, and relies heavily on Piaget, who is not primarily a learning theorist. On the social side the Report does carry into one of its most important Recommendations the now generally accepted realization that it is difficult to have a good school in a 'bad' neighbourhood. But it tends to play down the influence of social class, setting against this the importance of parental attitudes though these may in fact be the cultural components of class. There is no sociology of the school, no serious examination of the social role of the teacher and no consistent statement about the spheres of the teacher and the parent. All this reflects the confusion in the title – *Children and Their Primary Schools* – which implies that the schools are the children's, instead of the agents of a society of which the children are the as yet immature part.

These criticisms from the different studies basic to educational discussion all point to one thing: that the Report has gravely underestimated the positive role of the teacher, and of society in general, in the education of the next generation. It has done so from a fear of an authoritarianism and a constrained routine teaching that were accepted doctrine and practice in the past.

It is in the nursery and the infant schools that the 'new education' won its most outstanding success, and no one would want to return to the authoritarianism that preceded it. But with really young children the problem of being positive without being authoritarian is far easier to solve. As children grow older it is harder for the teacher to be acceptably positive while not being unacceptably authoritarian, and in this sense (although there is nowhere any sharp line of demarcation) the junior school and the lower secondary school have their own problems. Because of its initial wrong emphasis in declining to consider the positive role of the teacher, the Report simply projects upwards the philosophy of the nursery and the infant school and fails to put forward a rationale for the primary school as a whole.

It is this failure to consider the *positive* roles of the teacher and of society, and the consequential failure to establish a rationale for the primary school as such, that is the subject of this concluding paper.

Divergence between theory and practice

But at this point someone will probably say, 'Let us concede all that: but does it really matter? After all, our teachers have a certain amount of commonsense. They know perfectly well that life in a school cannot be just permissive; they know that we do try to interest children in things that ultimately we have decided are worthy of interest, though the image we use is that of growth rather than the old Procrustean bed; they filter the theory they learned in college through very practical experience, and the result surely is sound enough'. There will undoubtedly be some primary school teachers who read the criticisms made in these papers and feel just like that. But the point is not to suggest that they lack practical good sense. It is to ask whether we can be content with theory that so obviously has to be half-abandoned in practice because it does not fit real situations. Are we content with the legendary advice of the experienced teacher to the new recruit, 'Now you can forget all that stuff they taught you in college and get down to the real thing'?

If theory and practice are seriously divergent then one or the other, or both, must be at fault. As rational people we cannot be at ease while there is such a divergency. And it is not merely a matter of intellectual discontent because a formulation of experience is unsatisfactory (though this is not to be dismissed as a matter of the second order only). Practice is affected. If a teacher has not thought about treatment and contrasted it with punishment, his actions in class are likely to be impulsive and inconsistent. If he has not thought about the possibility that a certain pressure on a child to concentrate even though a part of a task seems boring may be justified (just as insistence when over the longer term there is neither joy or interest in it may be stultifying,) then again he will teach badly. Theory in education, as Professor Hirst has pointed out, is 'working theory', that is to say the kind of theory that enables one to develop a firmer understanding of what one is doing, and the reasons for it. If the theory is defective a working support disappears. This is only the first point in defence of the importance of the question we are raising in these papers. Others will emerge as we consider the matter further.

The standards of the old elementary school

However, having perhaps persuaded the successful practitioner that it is worth his while to read on a little further, we may now turn back to the Plowden Report and ask how the Committee got itself into this position of adumbrating a theory that does not fit what good teachers do. The fight against the old authoritarianism led us to neglect the degree to which the teacher's function must be positive, and has left us in a poor mental state to deal with the different problem of our own time. Our problem is not too much guidance of the young, but too little. This point is crucial. And all the fears we may have of being labelled 'authoritarian' must not prevent our saying it.

What we have to do is to solve in our own way the problem that the old elementary school did solve for its own time, though in a way that will not do in ours. Simply to pretend that there is not such a problem will not do. This is what we mean by saying that if the old elementary school and its authoritarianism represents the 'thesis', and the progressive permissive ideas of the reaction against it the 'antithesis', there is very great need now for a new 'synthesis'.

The elementary school of the years before 1914 was rooted in the English society of that day. Harold Laski hardly overstated when he said that the essential task of the elementary school was to prepare those who would learn to obey, the essential task of the 'Public' schools to prepare those who would give the commands (this, in deference to the changing modes of society, later became 'leadership'). Bernard Darwin said much the same thing when he characterized the essential quality of the 'Public' school man as 'readiness to become an officer'. All this no doubt is over-simple; but it is not wrong. The chief over-simplification is in omitting to add that the elementary school, in its teachers as well as its pupils, bred a certain kind of self-respect which was not without its overtones of independence. The elementary school, like society, was not static but changing. The tone of the elementary school of 1914 was very different from that of the old church schools of the middle of the nineteenth century. There was no longer crude talk of keeping people in their proper stations and of educating them simply for the lot to which God had called them. The teachers themselves had built up their Union and within an accepted social framework were increasingly self-respecting and self-reliant. The modes of teaching and learning, too, changed steadily. Mere rote learning, like frequent corporal punishment, grew less and less the norm. (Fifty years ago at my elementary school, if we had to learn the cotton towns of Lancashire off by heart, at the same time we could give the better part of a term to a 'project' and not be thought to be outrageously experimental).

What must not be forgotten, though, is that the old elementary school did have standards, standards of attainment (as the very word 'standard' for a form or class reminds us) and standards of behaviour and conduct. A great weight of authority was behind these standards, however many individual lapses there were. If the actual standards of attainment were criticized, if some of the social standards were already in the process of radical change, nevertheless that it was right for society to have standards and for the school to help inculcate these was not questioned at all. The teacher knew that he had a positive, not merely a permissive, function in the passing on of standards that society approved. The difficult thing to accept for those who were in the forefront of the fight against the old ways is that this last assertion is still true to-day and always will be. A too backward looking attitude, with warm thoughts of the victory that was won over the old *way* of inculcating standards, prevents our thinking hard enough about how society and the teacher can tackle this perennial problem in ways suited to our day.

The passing on of standards

There are many examples of this failure in the Plowden Report. Let us take one that is pedagogical and then come to more general matters.

Standards of speech. In the section on the teaching of English in the primary school the Report is under the influence of the struggle against formal grammar but goes so far in the other direction as to suggest that there is nothing normative to be thought of by the teacher at all. 'The test of good speech', it says, 'is whether any particular use of language is effective in the context in which it is used, not whether it conforms to certain "rules".' This is just not true; and I suspect that there is hardly a teacher in the country who acts as if it were. Of course formal grammar is something, so to speak, invented after a language itself. Of course a living language goes on living, and therefore changing. Of course a convention of a language may be broken, and this may be a sign of vitality. But to speak a language is to engage in a social action, and as in all social relationships there must be understanding among those in the society or everything breaks down. It is not a matter necessarily of logic, but of accepted, or at least acceptable patterns of speech. There is no logical reason why we should say 'Don't stay out in the rain' and the French should say 'Ne restez pas sous la pluie'. Whether one is in or under the rain isn't the point. The point is that in English the convention is to say one and in French the convention is to say the other.

To this it is no answer to say that if an English child said 'under the rain' his statement, though intelligible, would not be so effective because it would sound odd. It is the essential point about a language that it is a pattern of usages, not of solecisms. It is only because we do conform to such usages that we can communicate with each other effectively in the language we are using. What other rule does the Plowden Committee adopt in writing its own Report? Its language is conventional in the extreme.

This simple-mindedness about language echoes the Report's simple-mindedness about 'growth'. In this example too the Committee seem afraid to recognize the positive role of society and the teacher because they are still fighting a battle of yesteryear. The old dreary 'grammar' has surely gone, hybrid as it was, begotten by Latin grammarians on a living tongue in the dead shadows of a Victorian study. We can say, if we like, that we have thrown over those grammarians' 'rules'. We try now not to let formal rules kill imagination in children's writing. We even try not to make too much fuss over mistakes in spelling – but we don't say that there isn't a proper way in which a word is to be spelt, only that to get this right is less important than to use language vividly.

Once again this Report on the primary school has failed to distinguish between what is well enough for very young children and what needs to happen a little later on. The most important thing to encourage with young children is delight in adventuring with language. It is the expressive side that matters most, so that they will better realize their own experience. This continues to be important. But as children grow older something else has to be understood. This is the analytical use of language. This begins no doubt when a small child learns that words like 'hard' and 'soft', 'big' and 'little' describe opposite qualities. And he soon wants to learn to use them rightly, that is to say them in accordance with what indeed are 'rules'. You don't say 'hard' if you mean 'soft', and you perceive that there are two opposite concepts in the two words. But this has to go much further. When you go on from using words to express an experience to conducting an argument, or setting out directions for someone, or developing a concept, you are moving on to a different order of discourse. Such a use of language, as distinct from what might be called the expressive, is an indispensable tool in our social life. It should begin to be learned towards the end of the primary school. The great problem, as every teacher of English knows, is how to do this without killing the spirit that so often rejoices the teacher of children in the infant and the lower junior school. But it is certainly not enough merely to project 'spontaneity' upwards.

This failure to understand that education must be concerned with social usages in language – because, I repeat, of fear of a rigid formalism that has now virtually disappeared – is of a piece with the failure to understand the positive role of the teacher in other matters of standards. The general rule in language is that we should understand and normally follow the conventions of usage, but never to the point where the spirit is killed. If there is good reason for ignoring or breaking a convention, then we should ignore or break it. But otherwise we should not. (This will be felt to be hateful doctrine to those who have not thought the matter out and realized that this is in fact what they themselves do and would have others do). The same holds in the wider realm of behaviour and morals. It is *not* the school's business to imply that any kind of behaviour is as good as any other. It *is* the school's business, therefore, to encourage standards of behaviour and conduct that are good. (Someone again will say, 'How old-fashioned are you going to get?' But all the shades of Mrs Grundy must not prevent our saying this, for it simply is true).

Manners and customs. Now conventions of behaviour are of different kinds. Some are purely trivial, some are obviously more important. When I was an undergraduate and at a sports club dinner some poor scholarship boy (I was one myself) saw that his neighbour on the right had not taken any port and so passed the decanter back to him, the wrong way. I was astonished to see a former paragon of the College Boat Club, who had returned for the occasion, flush up and storm down from his high table seat to upbraid the poor youth. What on earth did it matter? The real point about preferring to pass the port the right way is that you know you are humouring a convention that once was based on a superstition that people seriously believed; and it is rather engaging that such customs should be humoured. But you do not let the bottom of your world fall out if some member of the company does not know that this is the way the game is played. It is of no practical consequence at all.

But if the scholarship boy had been aware of the custom and had deliberately flouted it, what then? If he had known his high-table man and had wanted to get a rise out of him I should have had a certain sympathy, for this is the only way people like that can be taught. But on the whole in matters like this, if you know what is the done thing, it is right to conform. This is not Luther nailing his theses to the door because he 'could no other'. Deciding what it is right to concede and what it is not right to concede is one of the hardest things of all to learn. It is part of our education, and very definitely part of social education in school as well.

Fifty years ago the short answer to the child's question 'Why must I (or mustn't I) do that?' was all too often, 'Because I say so.' We know now that this will not do, and increasingly will not do as children grow older. The authoritarian is the teacher or parent who will not give his reasons. The parent or teacher who will give his reasons may still, however, exercize some authority. Children are lost unless we do.

Morals and consensus. It was a great merit in Durkheim that he drew attention to the role of the teacher as the authoritative transmitter of society's standards to the next generation and that he saw that a new phase in social development called for a re-thinking of this duty. He saw the village teacher as well as the *professeur* in the *lycée* as standing for the values of the Third Republic in a French society that still had an overhang from an older regime. He argued that in particular the role of the teacher in moral education in France had to be radically reconsidered. Undoubtedly (though no one would say it was just because of a professor at the Sorbonne) the *instituteur* did come to stand for the values of the Third Republic in the France of the recent past.

To us Durkheim seems too rigid, indeed too authoritarian. So, in spite of a certain influence from new ideas, does the French schoolteacher of today. A new consideration is now necessary, in this country as in others, and this must take into account a changed situation in society as to standards and values. The task is indeed much more difficult now because the relationship between the schools and society is less clearly articulated than it was. This does not mean that the basic necessity for the teacher to have a positive function is less, only that the definition of the way in which this should be exercized is more complicated than it was.

There are still, of course, many insistences in our schools, but it is less clear than it was that these are the insistences of the generality of people outside, and in particular of parents. There is in this country an official insistence on religious instruction, but even those who wish to retain it are embarrassingly aware that what the school is commending as beliefs to the young finds little support in religious practice among the majority of parents. The intellectual, cultural and moral values that on the whole schools try to inculcate are not honoured by the commercial interests that seek the now much more ready cash of the young. Teachers feel that they are struggling without proper support from a society that officially expects them to uphold standards which in its unofficial, but real, capacity it denies itself. What, in these circumstances, is a teacher to do?

A rallying of forces is necessary. But where are they to rally to? The first need is for a survey of the field.

It would probably be useful to distinguish in a first approach between those standards that we could reasonably hope to be felt throughout a community and those which even in the best of societies would probably be understood and followed only by a minority. (I say, at a first approach, because one must consider how far the values of intellect and taste felt by a few can be fruitful unless there is some degree of common culture).

Now one's answer to the first of these questions will depend very much on the degree to which one feels that in spite of the things that divide us (such as religion) there is a consensus about the standards that in a broad way we should like passed on to the next generation. It has long seemed to me that the current laments about the falling-off of standards and the lapses of the modern young have obscured the degree to which there is such a consensus, not only among the public but also among the adolescent section of it. There is (and we often forget this) much more support from parents for so obvious a matter as school attendance than there was in the early days of compulsory elementary schooling. The trend for the young to stay on beyond the school-leaving age is a quite remarkable feature of our times. If a child does not want to go to school now he is recognized as virtually a psychological case, and we call his state of mind school-phobia. There are parents who do not back up the schools as headteachers might wish. But the broad picture is that parents want the schools, as they did not so uniformly a generation or two ago.

But what do they want them for? They want them first, quite simply, as a place where their children will learn. And if they want them to learn so that they will be better able to make their own way in life there is no need to take alarm at that. Parents also feel, in however undifferentiated a way, that schools ought to do something about inculcating good habits, however these may be defined. (Most teachers feel that parents expect this all too much and are ready to ask the school to do alone what parents ought to do in major part). If you ask the average parent what he means by 'good' his reply may be unsophisticated, but it will not be negative. He will make a reply that virtually always includes in some form the idea of being responsive to adult authority.

If you add to this the remarkable consensus we have in this country about what constitutes a good person you begin to get something on which a school can build. We have a strong sense of what is fair and what is unfair in behaviour to other people, and in the treatment of individuals by the community as a whole. We still have standards of financial honesty in public and private life that are among the highest in the world. We may not be quick in neighbourliness, but we put a high premium on reasonable kindliness and real good manners. (J. B. Priestley once said that if you could suddenly hear everything that could be said in a crowded underground train the most frequent phrase you would hear would be 'I'm sorry'). With us on the whole hysteria does not lie near the surface. In spite of the little snobberies that separate us in our groups one from the other, we are among the more tolerant of peoples. We are still an inventive people, oddly, although not notable now for mobility or excitement about change for its own sake. Money is by no means the only thing that earns respect in our society; nor are learning and artistic excellence held in neglectful contempt. There is not now the tradition of personal hard work over long hours through the day that characterized the Victorians and that is still more evident among some other peoples, and pride in craftsmanship is not perhaps what it was, but we are certainly not decadent in the sense that hard work is scorned or that standards in personal skill have ceased to be respected. These no doubt are all generalizations, and subject to many a qualifying footnote; but I think they are broadly true. They are qualities that we should want to pass on.

There is no reason to suppose that if our schools were a bit out in front of common practice in these matters our society would think it wrong. On the contrary it would think it right. But the development of these qualities does not just happen in the young. The parent and the teacher must feel that they have a positive role in helping them to develop.

There are, however, other areas which are more difficult. Sometimes a school may have to decide whether it will stand for certain values that the neighbourhood, or the general community, is not so sure about. Take, for instance, colour prejudice or racial intolerance. There is a pretty clear national conviction that this is wrong, but there are neighbourhoods where the influx of people who are clearly 'different' has been so large and so rapid that very strong feelings of antipathy have been aroused. A school cannot put right what its local community is every day putting wrong. But within the school a strong stand has sometimes to be made. Negatively, it seems to me, a school must stand absolutely against racial discrimination and prejudice; and positively it must do all it can to promote understanding and sympathy. On this its position must surely be unequivocal.

Another area of difficulty is met where, in spite of our general consensus as to what makes for a good man or woman, we find that opinion is very much divided as to what is right. Here it is surely the duty of the school (though more the secondary than the primary school) to promote tolerant but serious discussion so that the young understand the need to make up their own minds. A great number of important matters come within this area: sexual conduct, family relationships, capital punishment, the ethics of the profit-making firm or the factory floor, smoking and drinking, public support for the police, the citizen's duty to the state and to broader principles in matters of war and peace, and so on. Here the responsibility of the teacher is not to the opinions he may happen to hold (though he should in most cases state them, and always if asked) but to the whole procedure of rational, tolerant and informed discussion. That is the standard (rather than some one formal view) that he should uphold as a teacher.

Now how are these things to be done? There is, fortunately, no neat division here between moral and general education. Sloppy work, whether in arithmetic or the workshop, is bad. If the teacher makes it clear that he thinks so, he may on the surface be concerned with better arithmetic or making a tighter joint, but in fact he is also training character and helping to 'internalize' an important standard. The idea of fairness may find its place in a lesson on civics or current affairs. But its classsic embodiment for us is on the games field; and in spite of all the fatuities we have heard on that subject at Prize Days our tradition here is basically right and still potentially most valuable.

By and large the feeling is sound that it is bettter to let such standards be caught than to teach them by overt moralism. But I think we have gone too far in this. There are moments, even though they should be infrequent, when there can be the sharpest and most educative 'Pulling up' effect if a teacher or a parent says 'No, you can't do that. That's wrong.' We have become too afraid to use the words right and wrong. I was once present for an hour at a discussion in an honourable and enlightened 'progressive' education meeting that was discussing this sort of problem and I never once heard the word 'bad' used to describe behaviour. A child who behaved badly was never described as a badly-behaved child. He was always a 'disturbed' child. Now this is a sentimentality, born of the best motives, but still to be deplored because it isn't really honest. Of course it is wrong to come down in such wrath on a child who is behaving badly that he is filled with fear or guilt for the rest of his life. But it is not enough to say he is 'disturbed'. He may be behaving badly because he is disturbed, and to understand may be important. But it is nonsense to imply that there cannot be bad behaviour and that children may not exhibit it. They would hardly be children if they did not. And on occasion it is a good thing that they should know. If not, how is the idea of a standard as to what is and is not good ever to be implanted in their minds?

The problem of minority standards. These are standards that the school should help positively to be transmitted through the whole of society. But what can it do to assist the emergence and sustenance of those high standards that are unlikely to be attainable, or even felt, by more than a minority? Even in the primary school it will already be understood that only a few will be likely later to find satisfaction in reading T. S. Eliot or Proust, or will count Bach among their favourite composers. In this sense culture, high personal culture, is likely to remain the culture of a minority. Yet a minority culture in a social wasteland is likely to be sterile, and that surely the schools can help to avoid.

This is often a question of method. If you believe passionately, with a headmaster like Albert Rowe, in the education of the average child, you assert that he too has a right to as fine a command and as great an enjoyment of his native language as he can achieve, and if the methods used for the more gifted children do not 'take' with him then you ask what other methods may. Rowe has shown what possibilities there are if, in the right sense, you start where the average child is: with his eyes and his ears and a dawning experience that it delights him to realize through words. Then you find that there is a large range of good reading matter, some of it genuine literature and some of it trash, within his developing scope. The principle behind Rowe's work in English is not that you despair of standards with the less gifted but that you work towards good standards with an understanding of your children, with sympathy and with good sense.

Now this is very different from the interpretation one sometimes finds of this magic phrase 'Start where they are'. Start where they are and finish where they are too would seem to be the Plowden Committee's notion of teaching the English language. This is well-meant liberalism turning to cultural treason. Raymond Aron, in a recent discussion on quality in education, referred to an analysis in France of the young people who visited art galleries and museums and went to concerts of good music. It showed that most of them were at, or had been at, the *lycées*. He made the point that a continuance of our cultural achievements depended on education and that 'pop culture' was not a genuine alternative. Now this feeling that there are standards that it is important for society to preserve, and that a selective school can best do this is, as I have suggested elsewhere (in *Education and Contemporary Society*, page 135) at the heart of the best pleas for the retention of the grammar school. The reply to it is that this fosters such standards only for some fifth of our population and leaves the rest much more easily at the mercy of commercialized 'pop culture'. But Aron is right. No sensible teacher will just try to impose adult tastes or simply high tastes on the young, for to do so invites insincere acceptance or violent rejection. Let there be every sympathy for differences of interest, every understanding that 'popular' is not necessarily identical with 'bad', every allowance for tastes that are unconventional or ill-developed; but there must not be treason. The teacher who overdid the sympathy with her young for a well-known entertainer was asked, with perfectly fair logic at the end, 'Miss, do you love Elvis too?', and she was caught by the insincerities in her own position. The young should have the feeling that though they are free to say what they like yet the teacher has reserves because she finds satisfaction in things that she feels to be better, and that they might come to feel better too. Nor is it only a question of preferring one kind of thing to another – classical to popular music, for instance. There are such differences between what is good or less good within each kind, and for that matter there is no sin in entertainment either. A kind of tolerant sympathy combined with a communicated sense of honesty based on one's own standards is the only answer. Out of this could come a soil in which great art could flourish though not every one will rise to its heights, any more than Shakespeare's groundlings did.

The function of the primary school

How much of this is relevant to the primary school as distinct from the secondary school? A good deal, it would seem to me. In the broader matters of moral education it is important to remember that in the primary school children are passing from the stage where the authority of the adult is accepted almost without question to the stage where it begins to be questioned. This is a crucial stage in 'internalizing' standards of behaviour and morals. There has to be a combination of insistence and recommendation through explanation. The change is from encouraging the child to develop through happy and purposeful activity to one where he discovers that one can be happy in a community where there are restraints and begins to perceive that the restraints (in a good school or family) go hand in hand with his happiness, and the goodness of the community.

In the later years of the primary school the differences between the standards of the school and of the outside world also come into consciousness. Young children are remarkably free of colour prejudice. But by eleven or twelve, in a community where there is racial intolerance, the signs that it is being caught by the young may be all too evident. Again, by the later years of the primary school the appeal of the commercial forces that want to get at the pockets of the young will begin to be felt. A wise head teacher will talk with his or her colleagues about the attitudes that the school will adopt. If mere repressiveness (for instance of trashy printed matter) will not help, nor will mere permissiveness. A generally un-hysterical policy, but one that encourages children to start thinking about what they like best and why they like it – and what value they get for their money – is much more likely to succeed. And we should not be too afraid of exposing them to what on a narrow view is 'above their heads'. It is amazing how Shakespeare, acted not just read, can interest a class that could not give a paraphrase of a difficult speech with any detailed success.

What really matters is the picture that the primary school teacher has of his or her professional self, for this will communicate itself quite surely to the class and the school. It is the plea of this paper that unless the teacher pictures himself as acting positively, yet without the wrong authoritarian note which has happily almost gone, the standards that we want to be transmitted will not be transmitted as well as they might be. An inadequate theory of what you are doing is bound to let you down even though your practice may in some measure remedy the defects in your theory. Our criticism of the Plowden Report (leaving aside, as we have said, its often wise administrative proposals) comes to this, that in recent years although the practice of teachers has on the whole indeed been better than the theory that has often been given to them, there has been confusion and a resultant loss of power in the schools. By power we do not mean domination in the wrong sense; we mean power in the right sense, of positive educational functioning beyond being merely a catalytic agent.

The Plowden Report, unhappily, has not realized this need. It has left us where we were a couple of decades ago. No doubt, as Mr Dearden says, school education is a continuum. But if we have divisions according to age, and they are specific enough for us to say a year should be added to the infant school and a year to the junior school in compensation, then what should be the primary school's distinctive 'philosophy'?

I would say, very generally, that if the infant school is where the young learn through play, and the secondary school where they learn through work, then the primary school is where the transition from one to the other takes place. This must mean that it is in the primary school that the teacher increasingly acts, not just to put the young in 'learning situations', but positively to transmit standards that we want to be passed on to the young. If this is true, then a Report that for the most part simply projects the philosophy of the infant school upwards into the junior school is not going to help us very much. This unfortunately is what the Plowden Report has done. An opportunity has been missed.

Bibliography

AUSUBEL, D. P. (1961) 'Learning by Discovery: Rationale and Mystique' in *Bull. Nat. Ass. Second. Sch. Principals*, 45, 18-58.

BANDURA, A. AND WALTERS, R. H. (1963) *Social Learning and Personality Development*, New York: Holt, Rinehart and Winston.

BERGER, P. L. (1966) *Invitation to Sociology*, London: Pelican Books.

BERNSTEIN, B. B. (1967) 'Play and the Infant School' in *Where* supplement.

BLACKSTONE, T. (1967) 'The Plowden Report' in *British Journal of Sociology*, September, 1967.

BLYTH, W. A. L. (1967) *English Primary Education: A Sociological Description*, London: Routledge & Kegan Paul.

BOWLBY, J. (1953) *Child Care and the Growth of Love*, London: Penguin Books.

BRUNER, J. S. (ed.) (1966) *Learning about Learning*, Cooperative Research Monograph No. 15, Washington: U.S. Government Printing Office.

BRUNER, J. S., OLIVER, R. R. AND GREENFIELD, P. M. (1966) *Studies in Cognitive Growth*, London: Wiley.

BURNS, T. (1967) 'Sociological Explanation' in *British Journal of Sociology*, 1967.

CARROLL, J. B. (1964) *Language and Thought*, New York: Prentice-Hall: Foundations of Modern Psychology.

CICOUREL, A. V. AND KITSUSE, J. I. (1963) *The Educational Decision Makers*, New York: Bobs Merrill.

COTTERELL, G. C. (1967) 'Plowden, Reading and Dyslexia' in *I.C.A.A. Word Blind Bulletin*, 2, 9-11.

CROWTHER REPORT (1959) *15 to 18*, Central Advisory Council for Education (England) London: H.M.S.O.

DEARDEN, R. F. (1967) 'Instruction and Learning by Discovery' in Peters, R. S. (ed.) *The Concept of Education*, London: Routledge & Kegan Paul.

DEARDEN, R. F. (1968) *The Philosophy of Primary Education*, London: Routledge & Kegan Paul.

DEWEY, J. (1938) *Experience and Education*, New York: Kappa Delta Pi Publications.

FURTH, H. G. (1966) *Thinking without Language*, Glencoe, Ill.: The Free Press; London: Collier-Macmillan.

GORDON, W. J. J. (1961) *Synectics*, New York: Harper & Row.

GOSLIN, D. A. (1965) *The School in Contemporary Society*, New York: Scott, Foresman.

HARLOW, H. F. AND HARLOW, M. K. (1962) 'Social Deprivation in Monkeys in *Scientific American*, Offprint No. 473.

HORNSBY-SMITH, M. P. (1968) 'Parents and Primary Schools' in *New Society*, January 11th.

HUDSON, L. (1966) *Contrary Imaginations*, London: Methuen.

KERSH, B. Y. (1962) 'The Motivating Effect of Learning by Directed Discovery' in *Jour. Ed. Psychol.*, 53, 65-71.

LORENZ, K. (1937) 'The Companion in the Bird's World' in *Ank*, 54, 245-273.

NEWSOM REPORT (1963) *Half Our Future*, Central Advisory Council for Education (England) London: H.M.S.O.

O'CONNOR, D. J. (1957) *Introduction to the Philosophy of Education*, London: Routledge & Kegan Paul.

PARSONS, T. (1961) 'The School Class as a Social System' in Halsey, A. H., Floud, J. and Anderson, C. A., *Education, Economy and Society*, Glencoe, Ill.: Free Press.

PETERS, R. S. (1966) *Ethics and Education*, London: Allen & Unwin.

PETERS, R. S. (1964) *Education as Initiation* London: Evans Bros.

PLOWDEN REPORT (1967) *Children and their Primary Schools*, Central Advisory Council for Education (England) London: H.M.S.O.

PRIMARY EDUCATION IN WALES (1967) [Gittins Report] Department of Education and Science Central Advisory Council for Education (Wales) London: H.M.S.O.

SCHAFFER, H. R. AND EMERSON, P. E. (1964) 'Patterns of Response to Physical Contact in Early Human Development' in *Journal Child Psychology and Psychiatry*, 5, 1-13.

WALTROCK, M. C. (1966) 'The Learning by Discovery Hypothesis' in Shulman, L. S. and Kinslar, E. R., *Learning by Discovery: A Critical Appraisal*, New York: Rand McNally.

WILSON, B. R. (1962) 'The Teacher's Role' in *British Journal of Sociology* XIII, No. 1.

YOUNG, M. AND MCGEENEY, P. (1968) *Learning Begins at Home*, London: Routledge & Kegan Paul.